The Practice of Prayer

The New
Church's Teaching Series
Volume 4

The Practice of Prayer

Margaret Guenther

COWLEY PUBLICATIONS
Cambridge, Massachusetts

The title *The Church's Teaching Series* is used by permission of the Domestic and Foreign Missionary Society. Use of the series title does not constitute the Society's endorsement of the content of the work.

Library of Congress Cataloging in Publication Data:
Guenther, Margaret, 1929-
    The practice of prayer/Margaret Guenther
      p.   cm.   —(The new church's teaching series; v.4)
    Includes bibliographic references.
    ISBN: 1-56101-152-5 (alk. paper)
    1. Prayer—Episcopal Church. 2. Episcopal Church—Doctrines. I. Title.
II. Series.
BV210.2.G82   1998
248.3'2—dc21   98-25255
                                                       CIP

Scripture quotations are from the *New Revised Standard Version* of the Bible, © 1989 by the Division of Christian Education of the National Council of the Churches of Christ in the USA. Used by permission. All rights reserved.

Editor: Cynthia Shattuck
Copyeditor and Designer: Vicki Black
Cover art by Valerie Reilly, *Paisley Patterns*, from the Paisley Museum and Art Gallery, Scotland.

This book was printed in Canada on recycled, acid-free paper.

Fifth Printing

Cowley Publications
4 Brattle St. • *Cambridge, Massachusetts 02138*
1-800-225-1534 • *www.cowley.org*

Contents

The New Church's Teaching Series

Almost fifty years ago a series for the Episcopal Church called The Church's Teaching was launched with the publication of Robert Dentan's *The Holy Scriptures* in 1949. Again in the 1970s the church commissioned another teaching series for the next generation of Anglicans. Originally the series was part of an effort to give the growing postwar churches a sense of Anglican identity: what Anglicans share with the larger Christian community and what makes them distinctive within it. During that seemingly more tranquil era it may have been easier to reach a consensus and to speak authoritatively. Now, at the end of the twentieth century, consensus and authority are more difficult; there is considerably more diversity of belief and practice within the churches today, and more people than ever who have never been introduced to the church at all.

The books in this new teaching series for the Episcopal Church attempt to encourage and respond to the times—and to the challenges that will usher out the old century and bring in the new. This new series differs from the previous two in significant ways: it has no official status, claims no special authority, speaks in a personal voice, and comes not out of committees but from scholars and pastors meeting and talking informally together. It assumes a different readership: adults who are not "cradle Anglicans," but who come from other religious traditions or from no tradition at all, and who want to know what Anglicanism has to offer.

As the series editor I want to thank E. Allen Kelley, former president of Morehouse Publishing, for initially inviting me to bring together a group of teachers and pastors who could write with learning and conviction about their faith. I am grateful both to him and to Morehouse for participating in the early development of the series.

Since those initial conversations there have been substantial changes in the series itself, but its basic purpose has remained: to explore the themes of the Christian life through Holy Scripture, historical and contemporary theology, worship, spirituality, and social witness. It is our hope that all readers, Anglicans and otherwise, will find the books an aid in their continuing growth into Christ.

James E. Griffiss
Series Editor

Acknowledgments

I am grateful to the Board of Trustees of The General Theological Seminary for granting me a sabbatical semester, a gift of time and spiritual space that enabled me to write this book. I am also deeply grateful to Cynthia Shattuck and Vicki Black of Cowley Publications for their friendship, creativity, and wisdom.

Writing about God is tricky business in these days of heightened linguistic sensibilities concerning gender. For ease of style, I have primarily used traditional language in speaking of the creator-parent God, aware that "God created humankind in his image, in the image of God created he them, male and female created he them." All our words are an attempt and an approximation, for we "see in a mirror, dimly." God is Father, but the infinite and ultimately unknowable God is also much, much more. God refuses to be reduced to a pronoun. Given the limitations of language, I have tried to honor that truth and hope that I have offended no one.

I would like to dedicate this book to the memory of my father, Otto. And, as always, I am sustained by my husband Jack and his faith in me.

PART I

Spirituality and Prayer

Chapter One

An Introduction to Spirituality

What's in a Name?

I confess to being daunted by the title of this book—*The Practice of Prayer*. What arrogance to presume even minimal competence, let alone mastery of such a topic as prayer! To say nothing of the fact that religious bookstores are filled with shelves of books on how to pray—with words and without words, with rosaries and icons, with scripture and saints, using our imagination and suppressing our imagination. My own study has more than its share of such books, each one acquired in the hope that now I will finally get it right, that now I will become an expert pray-er. Should I really add another volume to the genre?

But I am writing about the *practice* of prayer. "Practice" is a reassuringly down-to-earth word. We practice because we are not yet perfect, because we know that we have much to learn. To be fruitful, practice must be faithfully sustained over a long period. Practice is rarely exciting, often not even interesting: anyone who has gained fluency in a foreign language or modest competence with a musical instrument knows that there are no short cuts. Practice can be tedious, and the prize is glimpsed fleetingly at best. When we practice we make mistakes, often the same mistakes over and over, until finally that particular challenge is overcome. Then we discover that our new level of achievement brings new challenges, and the cycle begins again.

Adults tend to forget how difficult acquiring and practicing new skills can be. We smile patronizingly on young children, whose challenges seem less stressful than our own, and yearn for the kindergarten days, when life was easy. Just as mothers are said to forget the pain of childbirth, we have forgotten the tedium, frustration, and challenges of the intense practice that has brought us to maturity. We have forgotten that the demands of each stage along the way have stretched us to our limits.

Our life of prayer is a life of practice. Sometimes we are stuck with boring finger exercises or daunting scales with six flats. Sometimes we are led with growing confidence through the tangled intricacies of a Bach fugue and are rewarded with a triumphant harmonic chord at the end that brings together all the disparate strands of melody, making some sense of what seemed troubling or meaningless in our lives before. Sometimes we look for beauty and meaning in the spiritual equivalent of atonality and dissonance. Sometimes we struggle just to get through "Twinkle, Twinkle, Little Star." The point is that we practice prayer faithfully. We keep at it. We never quite get it right—or if we do, we realize quickly that we have only reached a resting point, that there are greater depths or heights to be explored.

Sometimes we practice prayer alone, sometimes with others, sometimes with the help of a teacher. The practice of prayer is more than a program of devotional activity, the spiritual equivalent of twenty minutes on the NordicTrack or five minutes of toothbrushing and flossing. The practice of prayer is the work of a lifetime, touching every aspect of our life, from the search for identity to the challenge of vocation to the acceptance of death. It takes us through the heights, the depths, and the desert—to say nothing of the occasional swamp. When I was growing up a diet self-help book called *You Are What You Eat* was popular; I am tempted to call this book *You Are How You Pray.* How we practice our prayer makes a difference in who we are and what we become.

∼ The Spiritual Life

In my office there is a book on the shelf that I have never read. I cannot even remember now how I acquired it—maybe the person who used the office before me left it, maybe someone gave it to me, maybe I picked it up from a sale table. I have meant to read it, yet for years I have avoided it. It may be a wise and humane book, but the title scares me: *Am I Living a Spiritual Life?* How would I answer that question, I who forget to say my prayers and neglect to love my neighbor? I who get bored by long sermons and sometimes wonder whether God has forgotten me? I who get caught up in the minutiae of daily living and am chronically overwhelmed by faithless fears and worldly anxieties?

And what is a spiritual life, anyway? Surely it is the province of certified saints—preferably dead—or at least of people who wear special clothes and have religious titles. People for whom God is a full-time job. Of course, I have been a priest long enough to know that a stiff white clerical collar is not a guarantee of *anything*, and I have close friends in religious orders who have lovingly made it clear to me that they are fallible humans, albeit garbed medievally and adept in Benedictine chant. Still, who am I to aspire to the spiritual? Surely that is the domain of the unusually gifted or deeply pious. For most of us, the mundane is challenge enough.

And for that matter, do I even *want* to live a spiritual life? It sounds disembodied, not much fun, and surely difficult to sustain for long periods—especially when the weather is hot and humid or when there are impossible deadlines to be met or when my family is driving me crazy. Maybe, I think, I will postpone the spiritual life until I have more time, or when there is nothing much else to do.

My fear of the book on my office shelf is, of course, unfair; I have judged a book by its title if not by its cover. I am grateful for that title, however, for it raises an essential question, a question rarely articulated but implicit in the lives of most faithful people: *Am I doing it right?* And that question leads to others: What am I supposed to be doing? How does my professed faith relate to the rest of my life? In other words, what does the ten o'clock church service on Sunday morning have to do with reality? Does God know where I am? Or for that matter, does God know *that* I am? And does it matter?

〜 Personal Spirituality

Spirituality is in the air these days, all too often as something to be caught, achieved, or marketed. Certainly, "spirituality" is a difficult word with lots of baggage for many of us. It is a word that challenges us and sometimes makes us uneasy, for it is nebulous, elastic, and potentially dangerous. It is a word we often suspect of covering up loose thinking or of providing an avenue of private escape from engagement with the pain, need, and injustice in the world. Unfortunately, there is some truth in such assumptions, but it is only a partial truth.

It is important to remember that we all—even the most ordinary and least holy among us—have a spirituality. It may be bland, rejecting risk and adventure in favor of the safe and predictable, the spiritual equivalent of a tuna casserole instead of a challenging curry. Our spirituality can be selfish, destructive, or even daemonic, as we have seen in the example of Hitler's Third Reich, with its creeds and liturgies permeating every aspect of the nation's life, or the perverse spiritualities that united the disciples of Charles Manson and Jim Jones. Whatever its characteristics, every one of us has a spirituality, what Augustine called an *ordo amoris*, an ordering of our loves. What do we most cherish? What do we most desire? What is the treasure hidden in the core of our being? Our spirituality is not what we profess to believe, but how we order our loves. That ordering may be unarticulated, sometimes even unconscious, but the resulting spirituality pervades our whole life and involves our whole person. Our stewardship of time, energy, material things, and relationships to our fellow creatures reflects the way we express that ordering of our loves.

One way of identifying the ordering of our loves, of uncovering our spirituality, is to reverse the question and ask, "What would rip the fabric of my life?" This is a disquieting question, one most of us would prefer to avoid. But history—world history and our individual histories—reminds us again and again that the fabric is fragile and that the seemingly immutable can vanish in a minute. The media inundate us with stories of earthquakes, floods, hurricanes, and bombings. An automobile crash can end a life in seconds. The pathologist's dispassionate evaluation of a few cells can shift our identity from active, productive citizen to critically ill, perhaps terminal patient. For me, the power of the film *Schindler's List* lay not so much in its depiction of the cruelty of the Holocaust as in its implicit and forceful message of human powerlessness: our stability is only illusory, and order can be swept away by the forces of disorder in a moment. I left the theater pondering, "What would it take to rend my fabric, to strip away my essential identity?"

∾ Secular Spiritualities

I have used "spirituality" as a broadly neutral term thus far, not necessarily Christian or even religious. Western culture offers a variety of secular spiritualities. The spirituality of consumerism, for example, is all around us; we need only to look at the advertisements that bombard our eyes and ears. In an economy based on ever-increasing consumption, to want and to acquire has become a civic duty. This spirituality of consumerism stands in striking contrast to Benedictine ideals of sufficiency or the simple abundance described by the prophet Micah: "But they shall all sit under their own vines and under their own fig trees, and no one shall make them afraid" (Micah 4:4).

Similarly, our culture offers a spirituality based on the avoidance of pain: we have myriad ways of dulling the sharpness of physical, emotional, and spiritual experience. It is illuminating to walk down the aisles of a pharmacy. There is a pill for every ache and a remedy for every possible bodily discomfort, all readily available even without a prescription. Likewise, we can dull our feelings with chemicals and our minds with trivia marketed as "entertainment." If we work at it, we can achieve—at least for a time—near total anesthesia. More to the point, the work of achieving a pain-free state can be all-absorbing.

Then there is the spirituality of violence, endemic in the American soul, although most of us would be ashamed to acknowledge it. Many Saturday afternoons in my childhood were spent at the Westport Theater, where week after week I watched the national mythology crudely enacted. The cowboys always won in the end. The laconic Indians were occasionally noble, but more often they were cruel and treacherous. All of the men had weapons, while women were either absent from the scene or huddled anxiously around the margins. Now, in another age of myth-making, violence that is technologically more sophisticated dominates our televisions and our streets. I have yet to install one of the elaborate alarm systems that are proliferating in our neighborhoods, but the heavy iron bars on my kitchen windows remind me daily that—like it or not, willing or unwilling—I cannot escape the prevailing spirit.

These are just a few of our modern secular spiritualities, and they are all rooted in idolatry. They have their own gods and their own liturgies. Professional football's televised Superbowl is a case in point, with its vestments, ritual, celebrants, and congregation. During its liturgy there is controlled violence and real pain; studies tell us that domestic violence increases on the day it is celebrated. The altar call is a call to consumption on this holiest of days for the advertising industry. And for the viewer, the entire experience is one of anesthesia: sitting passively before the screen, eating and drinking, absorbed in impersonal spectacle. It reminds me of Ray Bradbury's futuristic novel *Fahrenheit 451*, whose drugged citizens sit stolidly before giant interactive television screens. They watch banality and are in turn watched. Theirs is a spirituality of nightmarish passivity.

∼ Christian Spirituality

For Christians, however, "spirituality" is not a neutral term. No matter how far we might stray and how confused we might become, the order of our loves is ultimately clear: if we clear away the extraneous—even those things that are "good"—step by step and bit by bit, we know that *ultimately* what we want and what we love is God. We may not articulate this ultimate love easily; we may live for years, even decades, unaware of its source but deeply conscious of our love for the good things of God's creation. I love my family, I love my work, I love words, I love books and study, I love the Hazel River in Jenkins Hollow, I love the noise and energy of the New York streets, I love my friends, I love ripe peaches—the list can go on and on. The exercise is like peeling an onion or, if your tastes are more elegant, like stripping an artichoke. Layer after layer is removed; and there at the heart, sustaining and nourishing all the other loves, is the love and yearning for God.

As Christians we know that our identity in Christ is our true identity. We know that the two Great Commandments shape and govern us: to love the Lord our God with all our heart, soul, and mind, and to love our neighbor as ourselves. When we observe both commandments and are mindful of their order and unbreakable connection, our spirituality becomes both contemplative and active. Our whole person is involved—heart, mind, and soul. We cannot separate prayer from work or leisure or play, and while we know ourselves to be sinful and finite, we also know that we are beloved children of God. The call to love our neighbor assures that we are not alone in this enterprise: just as there is no private sin nor private prayer, there is no such thing as a private Christian spirituality. Christian spirituality is a family affair: it is lived in the midst of relationships with God and those around us.

Christian spirituality, then, is intensely practical, earthed, and real, for it is the way we live out our professed beliefs. It is a spirituality of relationship: not simply our relationship with God, but very human, embodied relationships in the here and now. How do we relate to others, those people in our lives whom we love as well as those with whom we struggle and do not like very much? It is easy to profess love for an unseen God, but infinitely more difficult to acknowledge the spiritual component in our relationship with a rebellious teenager or an irritating fellow worker. If there is indeed a God-component in all human experience, our spirituality pervades—even as it is influenced by—the office and the kitchen and the classroom.

Further, our spirituality is reflected in our relationship to all of creation, not just our own little circle of people whose lives touch ours directly. This connection is made clear in the first chapter of Genesis:

> Then God said, "Let us make humankind in our image, according to our likeness; and let them have dominion over the fish of the sea, and over the birds of the air, and over the cattle, and over all the wild animals of the earth, and over every creeping thing that creeps upon the earth." (1:26)

"Dominion" is an elegant word that makes it seem quite clear who is in charge and who is not. But it is a word that carries responsibility along with undeniable power. A long time ago I heard a rabbi tell a delightful story of Noah's voyage in the ark. Predictably, Noah fed and watered the animals, but he also cleaned their cages. Anyone who has mucked out a stable or cleaned the henhouse knows that this is necessary but humbling work. It is physically hard labor, and it smells terrible.

To have dominion over all that God has created is to bear the responsibility of stewardship. Sometimes I catch myself equating God's creation with unspoiled (or threatened) nature. It is, of course, much more. As a city dweller I have learned to see God's hand in unlikely places and to see abuse and disregard as a violation of creation. Stewardship is more than a Sierra Club awareness of exotic endangered species; it encompasses our whole consciousness. Good stewards are also good servants, ready to roll up their sleeves and dig in, both to protect and to nurture. They are also ready to rest on the seventh day to enjoy the beauty and abundance of creation.

Relationship with our own deepest self is also fundamental to Christian spirituality. To know ourselves and then to embrace that self as our true identity in Christ is a major, primary task of the individual Christian. Julian of Norwich knew this long before Freud and Jung and long before our bookstore shelves filled with volumes on self-improvement and self-discovery. Julian wrote in the fourteenth century:

> For our soul is so deeply grounded in God and so endlessly treasured that we cannot come to knowledge of it, until we first have knowledge of God, who is the Creator to whom it is united....For our soul sits in God in true rest, and our soul stands in God in sure strength, and our soul is naturally rooted in God in endless love....And all of this notwithstanding, we can never come to the full knowledge of God until we first clearly know our own soul.[1]

To know our own soul is not a self-centered exercise. Rather, it is to know which are the idols that distract and divert us from God and which are the icons, the windows to God. It is to see clearly where our attention, energy, and loves are centered.

---

1. Julian of Norwich, *Showings* (New York: Paulist, 1978), 288-9.

This quest for knowledge of our own soul is not a problem to be solved or work to be done in isolation. As Christians, we cannot be spiritual Lone Rangers. We grow in self-knowledge in the context of community. Otherwise, we risk being caught in a fruitless circle of self-absorption or self-delusion. Our spiritual friends and companions in prayer, people who love us with detachment and see what we cannot, help keep us honest.

Finally, we know ourselves in relationship with God. This relationship is not static, mechanical, or reducible to a formula. Nor is it comfortable; it certainly is not one to be taken casually. The writer of the letter to the Hebrews reminds us:

> The word of God is living and active, sharper than any two-edged sword, piercing until it divides soul from spirit, joints from marrow; it is able to judge the thoughts and intentions of the heart. And before him no creature is hidden, but all are naked and laid bare to the eyes of the one to whom we must render an account. (4:12-13)

This is not a God of warm fuzzies or sentimental, private devotion. This is a God who makes demands. This is a God who knows his creatures, who sees them clearly. This is the God to whom we pray in the Collect for Purity:

> Almighty God, to you all hearts are open, all desires known, and from you no secrets are hid: Cleanse the thoughts of our hearts by the inspiration [the breathing-in] of your Holy Spirit, that we may perfectly love you, and worthily magnify your holy Name; through Christ our Lord. (BCP 355)

That collect is what Christian spirituality is all about. To withstand this scrutiny and to live in the presence of this

God to whom all hearts are open, we must ground our self-understanding and our growing self-knowledge in humility, the neglected virtue that simply means knowing who we are in the sight of God, knowing our place in the order of things. Such knowledge results, of course, in respect for the otherness of all persons.

More importantly, it fills us with awe at the otherness of God. God is God. I am not God. I can and must work diligently at my spiritual fitness program; asceticism, after all, is rooted in the concept of athletic training, not self-torture. But ultimately, I must rely on the action of the Holy Spirit. I still remember my relief when I learned in Systematic Theology I that it is *God* who saves us, not we ourselves. Awareness of this basic and quite simple fact makes all our ministries, lay and ordained, much more manageable. It also means that we are not alone in this work of living in and into the Spirit. It is not—ultimately—up to us.

✧ Growing Into Christ

If our spirituality is to be healthy, it must be ever-growing and willing to face risk and change. As our faith deepens, our icons—our windows to God—can become idols, false gods, if we do not let them go and move on to the new place where God is calling us. A beloved version of the prayer book or the Bible translation of our childhood or perhaps certain liturgical forms are good examples of this. The very words and forms and pictures that once opened us to God and God to us become static and ossified. They get in the way. We mistake them for God. Then our outworn idols need to be smashed or at least named and gently put on the shelf.

Without such a healthy, self-critical spirituality our striving in evangelism and outreach will be flawed. Our living out of the great commission to go and make disciples of all nations will be ineffective and hollow at best and destructive and sinful at worst. History offers us vivid examples of those times when Christians forgot who they were in God's great economy. The Crusades, the Inquisition, the persecution of women as witches, the forced conversion of indigenous peoples—all these cruel and destructive efforts reflect a tragically distorted spirituality that was unwilling to be self-critical. When we see the effects of clinging to idols, it is clear that paying attention to the state of one's spiritual health is not necessarily self-centered navel-gazing. Nor is it the avoidance of the work of evangelism or engagement in Christian community. Rather, it is a vital precondition to anything we may do in church or in the name of the church.

Tending to one's spiritual life is not an easy task. First of all, it can never be fully accomplished, for we are never done. Just when we are sure that we know who we are, we must begin again. Further, we are adept at deceiving ourselves about our spiritual well-being or lack thereof. Jeremiah, one of my favorite curmudgeons, reminds us that "the heart is devious above all else; it is perverse—who can understand it?" (17:9). Our avoidance and self-delusion are not necessarily "bad"; they may be quite attractive and seemingly constructive. If, for example, I can get very busy turning stones into bread, am I not being unselfish and generous? To be sure, I am so busy doing God's work that I do not have time to pray or talk with my spiritual director or even just quiet down and listen to what God might be trying to say to me. Excessive busyness, particularly in the service of a good cause, is an effective way of hiding from God and from our own deepest self.

We can also avoid exploring our true spirituality by shrinking from risk. It is easy to stay caught in an unexamined faith, suppressing our questions and denying our uncertainties. "We're just not meant to know" was the pious answer to most of the theological questions I dared to raise in my conservative midwestern childhood. It took me decades to realize that fidelity is not synonymous with passivity and that an inquiring mind is one of the gifts of the Holy Spirit. If we are to grow up into Christ, we must be willing to push out the boundaries and accept the possibility of change—not change in the immutable God who was and is, but change in our perception and understanding of who this God is and who we are in relationship to God. Growing up is never easy. The stresses of physical adolescence are well documented, but the pain and strain of spiritual adolescence is rarely discussed, possibly because we can avoid spiritual growth but bodily change is beyond our control.

The pain that change and growth can cause was brought home to me a few years ago when I offered a course on Julian of Norwich at an Elderhostel. The group had sat quietly and amiably through my opening lectures (although one woman announced that anchorites had to be crazy, no matter how much I had stressed Julian's wholeness and balance). But my discussion of Julian's God-imagery, particularly her engaging picture of Jesus as mother, pushed us over the line. "What on earth are you trying to tell us?" erupted an outraged elder. "Everybody *knows* that God is a *man!*"

The encounter saddened me. The week of the program was almost over, and there were no opportunities for real conversation—assuming, of course, that my distressed listener wanted to talk and risk further shaking of the foundations. I wish that I could have talked with her, not to convince her or to defend myself, but just to communicate somehow that our wonderful gifts of freedom and imagination come from God. I am convinced that God welcomes our questions and invites us to play. "Ah," I can imagine God saying, "you think that painting of me on the ceiling of the Sistine Chapel is my passport photo. It's a good picture, but guess again!"

I did not articulate it to myself then, but I can say now what I wanted to give to the woman I had disturbed: an invitation to trust herself, look deep within herself, and let herself be open to the mystery of God. I wanted to give her courage to let go, even for a little while. I wanted to invite her to join in the adventure of the spiritual life. For I know now what I knew all along: the answer to the question posed in the title of the unread book on my study shelf is a resounding *Yes!* Made in God's image and beloved of God, we cannot *help* but lead spiritual lives. We are spiritual beings. Implicitly, we are prayerful beings, even though most of us protest that we do not pray enough or pray in the "right" way. We are all yearning for God, a yearning understood by Augustine of Hippo in his prayer at the beginning of his *Confessions:* "You have made us for yourself, O God, and our heart is restless until it finds its rest in you."

So I am writing this book for the people who would never claim to be theologians but who have felt the tug of God. It is based on the premise that there is a God-component in our everyday experience. At times this component is readily apparent, manifest in moments of grace—a flooding awareness of God's goodness, a certainty of God's closeness. At other times, it is found paradoxically in a sense of God's seeming absence, that state designated in Christian tradition as "desolation." In all events, we live our lives in the sight of God, known and loved by the One who created us. Time and energy are the raw materials God has given us, and there is some spiritual significance in the most humble and the most glorious aspects of our existence. I find God present in the kitchen and on the subway, when I sit before the computer screen struggling to find the right word and when I loll in the hammock on hot summer days, content to listen in total idleness to the buzz of the cicadas. I suspect that it would be too intense if we were to live every moment conscious that we are held by God. But an occasional reminder never hurts!

This book is also based on the premise that everybody prays, whether we know it or not, and that each of us has a rich variety of prayer experience. Too often we let ourselves be locked into the belief that only prayers in the context of worship or certain words said privately at certain times "count" as prayer. Some of us pray with words, while others pray without words. Some ask boldly for God's intervention in the details of our lives, even the most trivial, while others pray more generally, for strength to endure whatever may come. Sometimes prayer comes easily and sometimes it is a wrestling match, rivaling Jacob's hand-to-hand grappling with the LORD at the ford of Jabbok. Sometimes we are uplifted, and sometimes we fall asleep. But as faithful people we all pray. Somehow. Even if we hesitate to call it "prayer" or are convinced that we are doing it all wrong.

I also hope that this will be prove to be a practical book, answering some of the questions you might have wanted to ask but have never expressed. Decades as a teacher have taught me that there are no "dumb" questions, and that the questions we hesitate to ask are often the ones that really matter.

There are many resources for learning *about* God: there are books, courses, and study groups on scripture, theology, and history. But to know the unknowable God is the impossible yet irresistible undertaking of a lifetime. To embark on that adventure is not to undertake a course in self-improvement or self-discovery (although both will inevitably occur). Rather, what we are about is the cultivation of attentiveness as we risk living into an openness to God. It is accepting the freedom that comes with letting go our defenses and living into the questions.

Chapter Two

Prayer as Conversation

Is Anyone Listening?

A good conversation is like a dance. The partners are aware of each other, attuned to each other, sensitive to nuances in tempo and rhythm. A good conversation with a friend—in contrast to idle chitchat with an acquaintance—allows space for pauses. There is no need to fill every minute, for there is comfort in the intimacy of shared silence. A good conversation is generous: each partner brings the gift of willing attentiveness. Listening is as important and as dynamic as speaking.

We take it for granted that God is listening to our prayers, but just to be sure we usually add a petition to our litanies: "Lord, hear our prayer." I catch myself wondering if God finds some of our prayers more interesting and promising than others. From my years in the classroom, I know that students at all levels are eager for their papers (even the badly written, shamefully overdue ones) to be read at once and commented on—favorably, of course. They cannot imagine that their teachers are not eager to plunge into the often dreary task. Does God feel that way about our prayers, I wonder? Surely not! As the words of the psalm reassure us, "The eyes of the LORD are upon the righteous, and his ears are open to their cry" (34:15).

God indeed listens to our prayers with loving attentiveness—though, to be sure, it does not always seem so to us. Almost everyone experiences times when God seems inattentive to what we have to say, if not entirely absent. Yet if we trust the promise of scripture that God desires an intimate relationship with us, we are impelled to communicate, to enter into the conversation of prayer. This conversation is a two-way street, however, and we need to do our share of listening. The question is, how do we listen to what God has to say?

I am uneasy when I encounter people who purport to have received direct, verbally concise communications from God. Elijah and the other prophets of Hebrew scripture can get away with proclaiming, "Thus says the LORD," or "The voice of the LORD came to me," but we are wary (usually rightly so) of our contemporaries who announce, "God told me that...." These may be the truly deranged—"God told me to kill my children"—or the arrogantly manipulative—"God told me that all gay people are damned." It requires amazing temerity to assume that we know God's will in minute detail and to dare to speak prescriptively in God's behalf. Holy wars, great and small, and unspeakable cruelty are the fruits of such hubris.

And yet throughout the centuries, including our own, there have been those highly sensitive persons who seem to have a direct line of two-way communication with God. I remember my feeling of envy the first time I read Julian of Norwich's *Showings*. I did not want to experience her terrible illness or to live out my life in the austerity of a medieval anchorhold. But how I wished that I could experience God's immediacy as she had! From her writings I could tell she was no crazy woman; she seemed very ordinary and down-to-earth. Why had she—like Teresa of Avila, John of the Cross, and Meister Eckhart, to name my other mystic friends—been so gifted? How do we tell the true mystics from the merely deluded?

The true mystics, those whom Evelyn Underhill characterizes as "person[s] with a genius for God" are gifted with heightened perception: inwardly, they "see" and "hear" with great clarity. Their words, unlike the supposedly divine messages reported by the demented or the demagogue, can be trusted, for "the business and method of mysticism is love....It is the eager, outgoing activity whose driving power is generous love."[1] I have found that most mystics today are hidden, and quite out of step with our age of high technology; earlier centuries may have been more hospitable to their special giftedness. Almost without exception, they are humble folk, not preoccupied with their own proficiency. They would be surprised and a little embarrassed to be labeled "mystics." We know they are true mystics because they wear their giftedness lightly, and their "driving power is generous love."

～ Paying Attention

Most of us lack the "genius" for hearing the voice of God that characterizes true mystics. For us ordinary folk, the sound of God's voice is likely to be more subtle, and we can miss out entirely if we are waiting for a booming voice from a cloud or some state of altered consciousness. Instead, we need to school ourselves to pay attention, to fine tune our hearing and listen for sounds that we might otherwise ignore. Sloth—spiritual sluggishness—is the natural enemy of such attentiveness. Constant awareness

---

1. Evelyn Underhill, *Mysticism* (New York: E. P. Dutton, 1961), 104, 85.

is demanding work, and it is tempting to ignore God's whispers, sighs, and nudges.

Our ordinary listening is—indeed, must be—selective. Flooded with stimuli as we are, there are simply too many sounds in the course of our normal day-to-day lives for us to handle. People with new hearing aids report that the joy of being able to hear human speech again is almost overshadowed by the confusion caused by hearing all the other noises amplified as well. They must master again the skill that we take for granted: sorting out the sounds and ignoring those that do not serve us. After nearly twenty years of living in New York, I confess that I can sleep through car alarms screaming under my bedroom window. Loud voices threatening violence do get my attention—sometimes. I am always surprised when visitors comment on our noisy nights. "But this is a *quiet* street," I protest.

When we listen for God selectively, we can be like teenagers, choosing to listen when and what we want to hear but otherwise remaining oblivious, turning our distracting inner music—whatever form it might take—up to maximum volume. If we let down our defenses, we might hear something that we do not want to hear, something that might challenge or reproach us, something that might force us to *metanoia*—to turn ourselves around and redirect our steps.

On the other hand, we can learn to listen selectively for God in a positive way by tuning out the distracting inner noises and letting ourselves be open to God's voice. We begin to listen by paying attention. This is hard work. It is easier and certainly more entertaining to yield to distractions. Our fast-paced, achievement-oriented society encourages *doing* over *being*, and devoting time and energy to quiet attentiveness can seem suspiciously like laziness. Even clergy are expected to be constantly busy; I have friends who feel guilty about praying on the job, unless they are presiding at public worship. God forbid, they should be caught sitting in their offices, apparently doing nothing! Nothing but listening for a whisper or a shout.

Television has shortened our already short attention span. I remember the thirty-minute or more sermons of my childhood, already mercifully short by my parents' standards; now anything longer than thirteen minutes risks losing the congregation's attention. We fear empty spaces in the day, just as we fear pauses in the conversation. Keep busy, keep moving is the order of the day. I know that I am in trouble when I take pride in my ability to do at least two things at once, even though it means I cannot give either my full attention. Outwardly, this makes me a high achiever: I can check off lists of tasks accomplished, letters written, books read, meals cooked, people talked to, and obligations met. Inwardly, though, I have defended myself against silence and space. Perhaps overly attentive to outer noises, I have made true listening difficult if not impossible.

There are those occasions when we seem to be attentive, but we are not really listening. This is a chronic condition in families and a source of jokes about husbands and wives. Inside and outside the home, our conversations are often superficial; indeed, convention decrees that the discourse at most meetings, receptions, and parish coffee hours avoid the depths. So inattention becomes a means of self-defense, a way of avoiding true conversation. It takes skill to appear raptly engaged while being a thousand miles away. Even as we yearn for the attention of others, we can be grudging in bestowing it.

God, we assume, does not play such games. Even when it seems otherwise, scripture assures us that God remains attentive to our prayers. The God who keeps track of sparrows and numbers the hairs on our heads is paying attention to us. Our part of the bargain is to reciprocate: to listen, to be open to what we might perceive, to attend. When we are attentive to God, we are willing simply to be there, patient and open to what we might hear. Such attentiveness does not come easily to busy people, living in a noisy world buzzing with distractions. To listen for God calls for firm intention and tenacity. We will never get it quite right, and sometimes the distractions will drown the voice we yearn to hear.

∽ Quieting the Inner Noises

Of course we listen with more than our ears. We listen with that inward organ of attentiveness that has never been charted in anatomy books. Silencing the outer noises that distract us is relatively easy: we can go to a quiet room, turn off the radio or television, close the window against street noises. Quieting the inner noises is another matter. They are like the tiny tree frogs, never seen but impossible to ignore, in the summer night in Jenkins Hollow. First one, then another, then a whole chorus fills the air. They drown out all other sounds—the last birds settling down for the night, the rattle of the river over the stones, even the neighbor's dog down the road.

Our inner distracting noises rise unbidden, like the song of the tree frogs, and envelop us. The frogs are beyond our control but we can get at the inner noises, swat them like flies one by one, and vanquish them. More gently, we can just ignore them and let them hop—or fly—away. Then we are ready to listen. Just as the prodigal son was able to return home after that moment of realization "when he came to himself" (Luke 15:17), we achieve inner quiet when we turn inward and return to ourselves.

The fathers and mothers of the Egyptian desert called this state of inner quiet *hesychia*. They understood the layers of sound that separate us from true quiet. So Abba Arsenius is credited with three commands. *Fuge!* Flee! Remove yourself physically to a quiet place, away from distractions good and bad. *Tace!* Be silent! Stop talking. *Quiesce!* Be inwardly still. St. John Climacus, a seventh-century monk and abbot of Mount Sinai, offered similar instruction: close the door of the cell, close the door of the tongue, and then close the inward door to evil spirits.

If we follow the teaching of either of these desert abbas, the first two stages of *hesychia* are relatively easy. It takes a little effort, to be sure, and might cause some social discomfort to stop talking when the air around us is filled with words. The third stage, however, is the truly difficult one.

I realized this a few summers ago when I spent several weeks in solitude in Jenkins Hollow. At that time, we had no telephone so there was no temptation to call friends and family, and of course no one could call me. We have no television there, and the radio offered limited possibilities. We have no neighbors nearby, so my conversation was limited to an occasional wave to the driver of a passing pickup truck. I confess that I was a little bit proud of my desert asceticism, passing whole days without speaking, and praying constantly. Then I realized with considerable chagrin that I was reading voraciously, devouring theological tomes as if they were *Gone with the Wind.* So much for inner silence! It was a good summer for study, but the desert hesychasts would have insisted that I throw my books into the Hazel River and then settle down to listen.

This kind of listening invites us to pray boldly, to accept new images for God and find our own language. Even traditional devotional language, which is essential for our common worship and unites us as Anglicans, can become a screen, helping us to hide our naked selves and to avoid the depths. Just as our words to God in solitary prayer should be *our* words, so can we expect God's words to us—however they might come—to be living, active, and real. We are familiar with hearing God's voice in scripture and the prayer book, in the psalms and in Gregorian chant. But the voice we hear when we let ourselves be inwardly still might be quite different and resemble none of these. I confess that for decades I assumed that God's native language was that of the King James Bible. Then I spent time with devout Lutherans who were sure that it was the archaic German of Luther's translation. We were both right, and we were both limited. In other words, God is multilingual and does not always use the language we are used to hearing.

And God's word to us can be surprising and unexpected, if we are willing to listen. I learned this years ago when I heard God's voice one day as I was walking down Central Park West in New York City. It was an inner voice; there were no sound waves in the air. I was fretting about a sermon that I was to deliver at the seminary where I was a student. It was an honor to be asked to preach and I was the first of my class to climb into the pulpit. It was the Feast of St. Michael and All Angels: my classmates and professors would all be there, listening carefully to each word. What if my theology was all wrong? What if my exegesis was sloppy? What if I missed the point of the readings? What if it turned out to be a terrible, boring sermon?

Then, right there on the busy street, I heard from God: "Who are you doing this for, anyhow?" "God," I thought, "is it really you? You've made two grammatical mistakes in one sentence!" Surely God would say, "For whom"! I know that psychologists could explain to me where my voice came from, maybe even why I had to correct God's grammar. But those words have stayed with me, reminding me for whom I work and to whom I must answer. They have become my talisman when performance anxiety gets in the way of candor and truth.

⁓ Encountering the Holy

When we listen for the inner voice of God, we are open to our imagination and intuition. We let go of the rational and explicable and befriend the unconscious. We let ourselves be vulnerable to the experience of God. Though it may seem obvious, this experience of the holy should not be dismissed lightly as pathological, trivial, or impossible; even in the church we can be all too quick to explain away the inexplicable. We can name a clearly mystical experience as holy without completely comprehending it.

At the same time, it is a misconception to assume that the experience of God must always occur in some state of altered consciousness or be an out-of-body experience. Certainly it *might* be, but most of us are blessedly ordinary folk who are yearning for God and who have experienced the holy in the midst of our ordinary lives—which is to say that we have listened for and heard God's voice through the words and voices and prayers of the church and of those around us. We may not always be aware of God's voice; we may minimize or dismiss the voice, and not tell others about it. Prayer is the most intimate of topics; for most of us, it is easier to talk about sex and death than to speak of our conversations with God. Sometimes we are afraid of being labeled "crazy" or being laughed at or shamed. We do not trust ourselves to articulate something so delicate and resistant to classification and measurement.

There are times when we do not recognize our encounter with the holy for what it really is, for our expectations are shaped by the religious ideas and vocabulary we have grown up with. Many of us are all too ready to discount our own experience because we cannot perceive the holy in our own lives. After all, we are so ordinary: we have no visions, we perform no miracles. We just get on with the work of living, doing our best and occasionally making a total mess of it. Can we really be on speaking terms with God?

That closeness is what we ache and yearn for. Not long ago I was with a group of friends, fellow Episcopalians. We were highly educated, psychologically astute, with impeccable good taste in matters of worship, not given to emotional excess. We were relaxing at the end of a long, hard day when someone, out of nowhere, launched into the old hymn "In the Garden." We all joined in. We all knew the words, even though the hymn has not and never will receive the imprimatur of the Episcopal Church's Standing Commission on Church Music. The room almost rocked as we sang, "And he *walks* with me, and he *talks* with me, and he *tells* me I am his own." Later we passed our spontaneous lusty singing off as just good fun, professing amusement at the sentimentality of the words and the kitschiness of the melody. Thank goodness, we were Episcopalians and above all that! Of course, we were not taking it seriously. We were just having a good time.

That incident has stayed with me. Under the guise of play, we had yielded to our yearning for intimacy with God, wishing for something as comfortable and soothing as the scene depicted in the bad poetry of the old hymn. We wanted to be sure that we mattered and were heard. We wanted a real conversation with a loving friend. If God took a walk with us in the garden, we would have no trouble listening; we would not miss a word.

Yet most of the time, we *do* have trouble listening. Besides the difficulty of stilling our inner noise, we easily overlook some resources, all suggested by scripture, that are all around us. God speaks to us in more ways than we might expect.

⁓ Dreams

One of the ways scripture tells us that God speaks to us is through our dreams. Yet many of us are uneasy with the idea that our dreams might be a reliable revelation of God, so it is tempting to dismiss them or to explain them away. When we move into the vast, rich realm of the unconscious, spirituality often defers to dubious science, and we slide into reductionism. We pick up just enough fragments of Freud or Freudian derivatives to convince ourselves that, ultimately, it all boils down to *sex*. This can make us afraid of our dreams: if we reflect on them too much and dissect them too thoroughly, they will reveal something about us that we wish to keep hidden. And, of course, they can! Or we can become fascinated by our dreams in a self-indulgent, navel-gazing way that—absorbing though it may be—can never lead us closer to God.

Yet scripture makes it clear that God uses dreams and speaks to us through our unconscious, that great unexplored, uncharted part of us. One of my favorite stories is of Jacob, a liar and a cheat who was spoken to by God through a dream of angels ascending and descending a ladder that reaches to heaven; then the LORD is standing beside him. This is a dream of proclamation and reassurance: "Know that I am with you and will keep you wherever you go, and will bring you back to this land; for I will not leave you until I have done what I have promised you" (Genesis 28:15). Some would probably dismiss his dream as the result of using a stone for a pillow, but Jacob knows that God has spoken to him. Upon awaking he says, "Surely the LORD is in this place—and I did not know it!"

His son Joseph is, of course, the great dreamer of the Old Testament. He courts murder at the hands of his brothers by flaunting his dreams and is sold into slavery. There is a message of caution implicit here: some dreams, however true, are better left untold. The mature Joseph continues to dream and to interpret dreams; his gift brings him to a place of honor and authority in Pharaoh's court. He becomes a powerful bureaucrat, saving the country from ruin. Reading with twentieth-century eyes, I wonder what would happen if the President of the United States sought out the most competent and creative dreamers in the country and then scattered them throughout the Supreme Court and the Cabinet! Yet like Joseph's brothers, we are not always kind to prophetic dreamers: the most notable dreamer of our time, who spoke the words "I have a dream," was martyred on a Memphis hotel balcony.

Joseph's namesake in the New Testament is also a dreamer, visited three times by God's messengers while he sleeps. In Matthew's gospel, Gabriel appears to Mary's betrothed in a dream to reassure him. Later, he is warned in a dream to flee from Herod, then told in another that he may safely bring his family out of exile. His actions are shaped by his dreams: he heeds their warnings and obeys their commands.

Jacob recognized that he had been visited by God, and neither Joseph ever questioned the validity of his dreams. Like them, we can learn to recognize which of our dreams are messages from God to proclaim and reassure, warn and guide us. Even as we remain respectful of our ordinary dreams—the psychological processing of the events of the day—we can learn to be attentive to symbols, stories, and images that speak to us of God, remembering that God's humor and gracious irony may color the dream so that it seems irreverent or even comic.

A gifted preacher told me of his recurring dreams, always set in the context of the eucharist, that reflect his struggle to understand and be faithful to the Word. In one the gospel book turned into a beautiful stone with barely discernible words etched on it. Another time the passage was in Spanish, a language in which he is fluent; it was easy to read, but he was impelled to translate as he read, never revealing to his hearers his role as mediator of the Word. In a dream of standing in the congregation to read the gospel, the words changed gradually from English to French (which he understands with effort) to Korean. "I knew it was Korean," he told me, "because I recognized the shape of the letters. But I couldn't understand the words." In yet another dream, the gospel turned into a giant cookie, rich and sweet, filled with nuts and chocolate bits. This baffled him until he recalled two verses from Psalm 119: "Oh, how I love your law! all the day long it is in my mind....How sweet are your words to my taste! They are sweeter than honey to my mouth" (119:97, 103).

Conversation with a good friend or spiritual director can help us recognize the God bits of our dreams, especially when they recur in different guises. Sometimes keeping a written journal of our dreams and our interpretation of them helps, so long as it does not become the tail that wags the dog. We can make such heavy work of our reflections! Like poems, our God-dreams are fragile. They yield their meaning most readily when they are handled gently, even playfully.

∾ Angels

Scripture also tells us that the voice of God can come to us through angels. Angels are popular. Bookstores offer dozens of titles, variously grouped under the rubric "Religion," "Self-Help," and most often "New Age." Angelic greeting cards proliferate, ranging from fine reproductions of major works of art to sentimental, bug-eyed cherubs who also turn up as pastel ceramic figurines. *It's a Wonderful Life* has become the secular Christmas story, acceptable to people who cannot quite believe in a God who becomes incarnate yet who long to warm themselves for an hour or two in the story of Clarence, the winsome, elderly angel who intercedes for the people in his care. Perhaps our secular holiday ritual is another instance of God's gracious irony.

It is time that the church reclaimed the angels. God's messengers in scripture are made of tougher stuff than their Hollywood or New Age counterfeits. Sometimes they come in dreams, sometimes during the waking hours. Gabriel is quick to identify himself, but others are chameleon-like. Did three men visit Abraham and Sarah by the oaks at Mamre, or was it three angels, or the LORD himself?

The story of Jacob's wrestling with the angel by the ford at Jabbok is similarly fluid. We are told that "a man" wrestled with him through the night, but when the struggle is over, Jacob knows that God's messenger was the LORD himself. There is nothing comforting about this encounter: it is a *fight*. God prevails, but bestows on Jacob a new name, a blessing, and a wound that will mark him for the rest of his life. Wounds and blessings are not mutually exclusive. To wrestle with God is to be locked in a painful embrace.

The consummate New Testament account of angelic visitation is, of course, the story of the annunciation, but over-familiarity has dimmed the terror of the event. My mental picture is of a Flemish angel with flowing locks, brandishing a magnificent lily in an opulent fifteenth-century room. The richly dressed virgin is a pale and boneless young woman who looks as if she has not done a day's work in her life. It is a beautiful scene, but safely distanced from any fear or upheaval, grubbiness or struggle. The real event of annunciation, I suspect, was not like that; rather, it was a shocking event with terrifying implications. Mary was right to be troubled and perplexed: Gabriel has proclaimed the impossible, and her life has been turned upside down.

His greeting to Mary is typically angelic: "Do not be afraid." This reassurance alone is an indication that something momentous is to follow. Just as Jacob's wrestling match with God left him with a painful limp but ultimately blessed, indeed transformed, Gabriel's visit to Mary leaves her both blessed and wounded. The elderly prophet Simeon understood the depth of her wound, when he warned Mary at the presentation of Jesus in the temple in Jerusalem, "A sword will pierce your own soul too" (Luke 2:35). Gabriel's "Fear not" makes it clear that under the circumstances any rational person would be scared to death. What we cannot know and what the angel is trying to impart is this: the encounter with the terror of God does not destroy us; rather, it transforms us. The reassuring "fear not" reminds us that we might be sorely tried and will most certainly be changed, but we will not be overcome.

When I meditate on the annunciation and try to find my place in it—for I am convinced that we all experience our own *small* annunciations—I wonder what I would do if I found an angel waiting in my kitchen as I burst through the door, already late in starting dinner. Or lounging in my study when I need to write a lecture for tomorrow morning. Or already sitting in the taxi when I am on my way to the airport. I would be tempted to say, "But you haven't made an appointment. You should have called first. I'd love to oblige, but this just isn't a good time. Maybe later...." But annunciations cannot be scheduled in advance.

The annunciations that come to us do not always look or feel like good news. Indeed, they may feel like blows or set-backs, interruptions and intrusions into our tidy, well-planned lives. Occasionally the news is joyous and clear, but the annunciation can take the form of downright bad news: illness, rejection, bereavement, seeming loss and waste. The angel—whatever form the bearer of tumultuous tidings might take—rarely carries a lily and practically never appears at a convenient time or place. Like Mary, as I imagine her, we would be quite happy to continue in our decent ordinariness. And yet the greeting comes: Hail, O favored one. Make a place for him within you. Get ready for your tranquility to be shattered. Put yourself aside, let your life be changed. And we answer: How shall this be? And maybe we really mean: Why me? Isn't it enough that I'm a fairly good person who plays by the rules and doesn't make trouble? Life is a great deal smoother if we manage to ignore our own annunciations. Maybe if we do not look up, the angel will just go away quietly.

I have loved the story of the annunciation since early childhood and thought that I knew it thoroughly. Yet only recently did I realize the impact of the final, simple sentence: "Then the angel departed from her" (Luke 1:38). Gabriel delivers the message and then leaves. How much easier it would have been for Mary if he had promised, "I'll be right here if you need me." Yet this is not the nature of divine messengers as they appear in scripture: they accomplish their mission and leave the recipient to deal with their cataclysmic tidings. This practice is in sharp contrast to the concept of guardian angels, a relatively recent devotional fashion from the early seventeenth century now seeing renewed popularity. Scriptural angels like Gabriel, who deliver their stunning messages and then leave, would be sadly out of place in the sentimental pictures of children walking through dark woods safely herded by white-robed winged figures.

The big question, of course, is how do we recognize the angels who come to us in our everyday lives? They are easy to identify in works of art, in stained glass windows and Christmas cards. But how many do we miss in the ordinary course of our days because of our inattention or willful resistance? The writer of the letter to the Hebrews reminds us that we never know where they might turn up: "Do not neglect to show hospitality to strangers, for by doing that some have entertained angels without knowing it" (13:2).

I like to think about angels in the subway, which is my desert place. One morning I stood at the bottom of the grimy stairs in the 23rd Street station and thought, like Jacob, "How awesome is this place! This is none other than the house of God, and this is the gate of heaven." It was not a vision, but the words were suddenly and powerfully in my mind. "Why not?" I thought. "It's no less likely a spot to see angels ascending and descending than a rocky patch of desert." Since then, I have been on the lookout. Angels have no dress code or standard of grooming, as far as I know, so why not see them in the subway?

∽ Prophets

Scripture also tells us that God speaks to us through his prophets. As a group, they are not generally comfortable, attractive people. I enjoy listening to prophets when they say what I like to hear (that is, when their target is someone other than me), but I prefer to tune them out when they threaten my comfort. Prophets can expect to be unpopular, to be opposed and even killed if they persist in their candor.

The quintessential prophet in scripture is John the Baptist. I have to confess he is not my favorite saint, although I was ordained on his feast day. There are so many others I find more congenial—gentler folk in the Christian calendar. John the Baptist is uncompromising and tough. In icons he is usually depicted as fierce, shaggy, and wild-eyed. In Matthew's gospel he is bizarre and cantankerous, coming out of the wilderness to upbraid the people who have sought him out and who probably felt they were doing the best they could. But as Jesus said of John, "What did you go out into the wilderness to look at? A reed shaken by the wind? Someone dressed in soft robes?.... What then did you go out to see? A prophet?" (Matthew 11:7-9). It is clear from his words that a prophet is to be taken seriously as a messenger of good news—no soft robes from royal palaces here. And the prophet must be a person of inexorable integrity, not a reed shaken by the wind. A true prophet, in other words, is a figure of ferocious love.

Almost by definition, prophets are not comfortable people. It is in their very nature to make us uneasy. Not because they can foretell the future—they are not fortune tellers—but because they insist that we look clearly at the present, at where and how we are right now. They do not come among us to make us feel good, that we belong or that we alone are the custodians of the truth. They come among us to shake us up. These prophets are among us now, even though they rarely look like the icons of John the Baptist or the pictures from our Sunday school books. Sometimes, though not often, they are easy to recognize, even though we might prefer otherwise. Each generation has its unmistakably prophetic voices.

In our time, Bishop Desmond Tutu of South Africa is such a prophet. He has angered and unsettled many Western experts who are unwilling or perhaps unable to let the simplicity of the gospel slice right through economic and political systems and theories. At the same time, he has angered and unsettled the more radical of the black South Africans who cannot comprehend his commitment to nonviolence and his ability to love white people as well as black. With his disarming smile—the polar opposite of John's fierceness—he has made us look hard at ourselves and at the conditions we condone.

Similarly, Gandhi—a short man with big spectacles and a skimpy cotton *dhoti*—confronted the injustice of British rule in India and prevailed. Dorothy Day and Mother Teresa, two strong women who, I suspect, were not always easy to get along with, lived passionately and prophetically among the poor whom they served, becoming voices for the voiceless. Rosa Parks simply refused to sit in the back of the bus. She did not set out to change the world that day, but her stubborn refusal to yield one more time to the injustice of segregation moved her into the ranks of the prophets.

Other prophets among us are less obvious and less visibly holy. Indeed, they are not so much prophets as prophetic presences. Living in a large city, I am constantly shaken out of my complacency by the presence of the marginalized, those people whom we would push to the edges because they are blemishes on our landscapes. They are often passive folk, incapable of concerted action and sometimes even resistant to those who would be their advocates. Yet their very presence is prophetic, challenging, even accusing—without their uttering a word. There are times when even the most tenderhearted and compassionate find themselves thinking, "If only the poor, the homeless, the addicted, the despairing and desperate, the violent, the hopelessly suffering would just go away—then we could persuade ourselves that the Kingdom has already arrived."

So it is a challenge to see Christ's silent prophets around us, especially in those who are different from us and who seem beyond our compassion. It is a challenge to see his prophet in the person lying on the sidewalk grating, filthy and perhaps unreachable because of addiction or mental illness. It is a challenge to see Christ's messenger in the person dying of AIDS, at least so long as that person is a faceless stranger to us. It is a challenge to see Christ's prophet in the desperate young men whose life of violence on the streets may lead to a life of caged violence in an overcrowded prison. It is a challenge to see his messengers in the forgotten aged, who are frail and immobile, no longer "productive" in our product-oriented culture, sitting in rows of wheelchairs, waiting for dinner and waiting to die. It is risky to let ourselves see them and hear them. Our world could be turned upside down.

Dreams, angels, prophets—and silence. Our multilingual God speaks with many voices. Listening for God might have been easier for the abbas and ammas of the Egyptian desert or for the self-denying Cistercians of the Middle Ages. Most of us, however, do not live in desert solitude or the stark austerity of a medieval monastery. To listen for God is to be engaged in a countercultural enterprise, for much in our daily lives works against the patient labor of attentiveness. Our world is noisy, seemingly addicted to sound and distraction. Our world is busy; wasting time is one of our national sins. Yet attending to the holy is slow work, a work of gradual growth and fruition rather than measurable production or conquest.

To live in this state of attentiveness demands comfort with surprises and open-endedness, for God is ultimately unknowable. In this life we see in a dim mirror, through a dark glass. We need each other in this work. Just as the old priest Eli helped the child Samuel to understand what he was hearing, we can help each other toward awareness of the God-component, the bits of holiness embedded in our everydayness. We can hear the answers to our prayers in unlikely places and circumstances, in what we "always knew," in familiar words that almost spring from the page alive with new meaning, in the chance words of friends or strangers.

It helps to pay attention. Are you listening?

Chapter Three

Varieties of Prayer

Does What I Learned in
Sunday School Still Count?

When as a spiritual director and priest I meet with people to talk about their lives, prayer is often explicitly and always implicitly at the heart of the conversation. Yet I almost always hear stories of guilt or inadequacy: I'm not praying enough. Or even more distressing: I'm not praying right. We seem to assume that there is a correct or prescribed way to pray—usually involving posture, setting, and a lofty vocabulary—and that everyone else has it figured out and is doing it better. Most of us think of prayer as a task to be accomplished, and we are convinced we do not measure up. When the report cards are handed out up yonder, the best we can expect is a B– (after grade inflation) with the Instructor's comment, "Margaret (or Joe or Sally) is not working up to her full potential. With a little more effort, she can raise her grade in the next marking period." As Christians we know that prayer is something we are supposed to be doing; Paul even exhorted the Thessalonians (and, I am sure, everyone else whom he encountered) to pray without ceasing. Yet what *is* prayer? And how do we do it?

Jesus himself teaches us that prayer is an essential part of our spiritual life. As a faithful Jew, he engaged regularly in corporate prayer and was steeped in the liturgy, as we can see from the many stories of his presence in synagogues and in the temple in Jerusalem. Luke tells us, for example, that when Jesus returned to Nazareth early in his ministry "he went to the synagogue on the sabbath day, as was his custom" (4:16). Jesus is also our model for personal prayer: again and again, the gospels tell us, he goes apart to a quiet place alone to pray. Particularly in Luke's gospel, we see a rhythm of intense periods of teaching and healing followed by periods of withdrawal to pray, sometimes alone and sometimes with his friends. Even people who profess never to pray can understand Jesus' last hours of solitary prayer before his arrest, when, alone in the darkness, he begs to be spared. All of us have prayed our small versions of Gethsemane at one time or another. Even from the cross, Jesus quotes from the psalms, the school of prayer for Jews and Christians through the ages: "My God, my God why have you forsaken me?" and "Into your hands I commend my spirit" (Psalm 22:1; 31:5).

Jesus also comes to us as a teacher of prayer, as well as an example. Luke tells us: "He was praying in a certain place, and after he had finished, one of his disciples said to him, 'Lord, teach us to pray, as John taught his disciples'" (11:1). The Lord's Prayer, uniting Christians throughout space and time, follows. In the Sermon on the Mount Jesus teaches his disciples to pray simply and in secret, not to flaunt their piety or "heap up empty phrases" (Matthew 6:5-8). And a number of his parables concern prayer: we are to persevere in prayer as a hungry friend continues to knock at the door until his request is granted (Luke 11:5-13).

Clearly, prayer is something we as disciples of Jesus are supposed to be taking seriously. Yet prayer is something we continue to struggle with, despite Jesus' teachings and powerful example. What would he think of all our books and pamphlets on what prayer is, our many classes teaching us methods of how to pray? Sometimes I can imagine him saying, "Why are you making such hard work of it? Don't you *get* it?" Surely the art of prayer is both infinitely simpler and infinitely more profound than we make it out to be. And yet all too often we are afraid to let go and plunge in.

∾ The Practice of Prayer

It is hard to find even a nominal Christian who is against prayer, although we may be uneasy talking about our own practices and embarrassed when we are "caught" at prayer. Comfort with spontaneous public prayer does not come easily to many, at least not to most Anglicans. But everyone agrees: prayer is a *good* thing to be treated with reverence, rather like motherhood, the flag, and kindness to animals.

I suspect, however, that we do more talking *about* prayer than actual praying. Many of us remain stuck at the level of rote recitation of prayers from our childhood. I recall signing off for the day each night as a child by rattling off "Now I lay me down to sleep," and then falling into untroubled sleep, feeling if anything a little safer since I had turned everything over to a Grandfather God somewhere in the sky. It is easy to stay in a comfortable rut; an unexamined faith is clearly less disturbing than an active, evolving one. Yet if our prayer is to be vital, it will be more than saying certain words at certain times.

This is not to minimize the importance of liturgical prayers or the comfort of familiar words that are etched on our spiritual hard disks. Prayer is a matter of "both/and" rather than "either/or." For the most part, our times of corporate prayer will be predictable, structured by the daily offices or eucharistic liturgies of the prayer book. *The Book of Common Prayer* is a vital cornerstone of our Anglican identity, and the prayers it contains undergird our spirituality. Regular, liturgical prayer in the midst of community reminds us that prayer is not dependent on how we feel, even though emotional highs or lows can force us into prayer. And our common prayer provides the foundation for our more personal prayer, when we let go of the book and permit ourselves to be spontaneous. We find our own ways and words—or we let go of words altogether. In candid conversation with God we are open to risk, willing to follow the leading of the Spirit.

True prayer, whatever outward form it might take, is first and foremost a condition of loving attentiveness to God in which we find ourselves open and receptive to who we are in our deepest selves. As Ann and Barry Ulanov state in their wise book *Primary Speech*, "In prayer we say who in fact we are—not who we should be, nor who we wish we were, but who we are. All prayer begins with this confession."[1] Our confession of the truth of who we are at this moment might be self-deprecating: "Dear God, I'm a hopeless mess today. I'm a fraud." Or dramatically self-accusing: "I have murder in my heart." Or it might be a glorious shout of jubilation: "Good God, I like the way I look and feel today!"

It is simultaneously a great relief and a challenge to lay aside our masks and postures and to be nakedly ourselves. We approach such openness in our relationship with loved

---

1. Ann and Barry Ulanov, *Primary Speech: A Psychology of Prayer* (Atlanta: John Knox Press, 1982), 1.

ones and aspire to it in spiritual direction. In prayer, however, our hearts are completely open and all our desires are known to God. We cannot hide, even if we want to. We can, however, delude ourselves that we are putting up an attractive and plausible front, not unlike Peggy, the decrepit family dog of my childhood who would cover her face with her paws and assume no one could see her. It can be deeply frightening to be so exposed to the God to whom "all hearts are open, all desires known, and from whom no secrets are hid" (BCP 323), but we also know that prayer involves us in an intimate relationship with a loving God. We are not casting sacrifices into a volcano to placate an angry God demanding payment for sin or promising a disapproving God that we will be better children tomorrow—although we all pray sometimes as if we were. Rather, we are addressing God intimately as the One who made us, loves us, and keeps us.

Whether we pray together in the liturgy or in solitude in a private space, we are always praying in company: there is no such thing as *private* prayer. After all, when in the Lord's Prayer we address God as *our* Father, we are acknowledging that there are other children in the family. If we have the same father, they must be our brothers and sisters. I confess that there are times when I would like to be an only child, but such a wish is not only selfish, it is impossible. When we pray we are part of the family. When we pray, we participate in the Christian community, past, present, and future.

Most of our prayer falls into the five categories we learned about in Sunday school or confirmation class: adoration, thanksgiving, confession, intercession, and petition. These categories of prayer are still useful, and they bear our revisiting them as adults.

～ Adoration

In prayers of adoration, God's majesty takes our breath away. We have all prayed prayers of adoration at some time in our lives, even avowed atheists: the sight of a brilliant sunset, a summer storm, a grimy city made clean and silent by a fresh snowfall, the exquisite perfection of an insect or flower can elicit a gasp of appreciation from even the most hardened among us. The beauty of the world around us and the contemplation of nature can evoke feelings of awe within us, and sometimes of terror as well. When I visit my daughter, I am fascinated by the Oregon coast but scarcely comfortable with it: the huge, jagged rocks and powerful, mysterious waves frighten rather than invite. Yet somehow it is reflective of one aspect of God, a tiny picture of overwhelming force and seeming chaos. Similarly, the sinuous muscularity of the coiled rattlesnake I encountered last summer by the woodpile in Jenkins Hollow reflected the beauty and precision of creation—though it was hard to remember to pray a prayer of adoration rather than panic as I scuttled out of its range.

God's creation—known in Christian tradition as the Book of Nature—is a valuable text for us to read of the majesty of God. The approach to prayer through contemplation of the wonders of creation is an important strand of the Christian tradition. Thus Paul writes in his letter to the Romans: "Ever since the creation of the world [God's] eternal power and divine nature, invisible though they are, have been understood and seen through the things he has made" (Romans 1:20). Through the beauty and intricacy of the natural world we come to understand the One who created all things, and to stand in awe of God.

And this creator God has made many things besides the world of nature. For some of us, music can be a pathway to the prayer of adoration. As a musician friend observed, "If

God is this beautiful, nothing else matters; just knowing that this beauty exists somewhere is enough." For others God is manifest in poetry, painting, or sculpture. Recently I sat with a soul-friend—the kind of friend with whom no words are necessary—in a dimly lit museum gallery contemplating a Romanesque madonna, carved centuries ago from a giant block of birch. She was simultaneously simple and majestic, heartbreakingly sad and yet hopeful. I rejoiced that Janet and I did not need to speak. We simply sat in the darkness of a winter afternoon. The artist's name is long forgotten, but as St. Paul would acknowledge, the divine nature and eternal power of God, invisible though they are, could be understood and seen through this thing God had made through the hands of an unknown woodcarver.

Adoration is not a cozy kind of prayer. It is a prayer that humbles us even as it exalts God. It reminds us of our place in the order of things, that we are dust and to dust we shall return. We show adoration with our bodies as well as our words when we bow as we recite the *Sanctus* in the eucharistic prayer: "Holy, holy, holy Lord, God of power and might." Spiritually if not always physically, we adore God on our knees. One of my favorite postures of adoration, practiced only in the solitude of Jenkins Hollow, is flat on my back in the grass, looking into the intense blueness of the summer sky through the scraggly branches of the big walnut trees that hold up the sagging clothesline. It is a glimpse of the infinite and the unknowable. Spiritually, at least, I am on my knees.

Adoration calls for a heartfelt letting go of all our pretensions and recognizing our own nothingness, though this healthy recognition of our limitation is *not* the same as wallowing in self-deprecation. Our capacity for adoration is diminished if not lost when we acquire the inhibitions and reserve of so-called maturity. It is perhaps a good thing that we grow past the stage where we fall easily in love; what is delightful or at least predictable in adolescents is disconcerting in adults who have taken on substantial responsibilities. But instead of losing our capacity for captivation, would it not be wonderful if it, too, grew up into maturity, just as adults grow past easy infatuation into something deeper?

When I took the General Ordination Examination at the conclusion of my seminary studies, I was trying to express this capacity for captivation in my answer to a question about the love of God. I wrote something to the effect that, if we loved God with our whole hearts, it would be as all-consuming as our first adolescent crush, when we could totally lose ourselves gazing at the beloved across a classroom or when a chance encounter and a few words transformed the whole day. My answer did not go down well with the readers of my exam, who chided me for being inappropriate and distracting. They did not specify distracting to *whom*, but I clearly made them uneasy. Their disapproval has stayed with me over the years and convinced me that I was right, even though I failed to express clearly what is inexpressible: the intensity of adoration that most of us cannot sustain but can at least experience fleetingly. In my response to the question, I had crossed the line separating the academic and theoretical from the dangerous territory of mystical experience. If we let down our guard, God can overwhelm us, captivate us, absorb us. It is adoration that puts blood and passion into our faith.

∽ Thanksgiving

Prayers of adoration often lead naturally to thanksgiving, for awareness of God's presence and action in our lives invites gratitude. Yet it is hard to say "thank you" except in a perfunctory, social sense—when you open the door for me, bring me a cup of tea, or help me in some small way. Sometimes we cannot find the words: saying "thank you" over and over seems shallow and repetitive when we want to express gratitude from our very depths. I love it when I hit upon the absolutely *right* present for a young child. It may have cost very little or nothing at all in dollars and cents, but it is received as a treasure. The child's "thank you" might take the form of a radiant smile, a total-body wiggle of delight, or an ecstatic sigh. Something is spoiled when a well-meaning parent interjects, "Now say 'thank you' for the nice present." I understand the necessity of teaching good manners, but it is painful to see the exuberance of true gratitude give way to a shamed and mechanical mumble of the "right" words.

Thanksgiving is also difficult because to be truly grateful forces us to acknowledge our smallness, helplessness, and neediness. To be thankful is to be indebted, and we live in a society that makes a virtue of independence. So we say "thank you" almost mechanically in response to minor courtesies, but very often would rather not acknowledge our deep debts to those—known and unknown—who bring their gifts, their skill, and their work to maintain us, body and soul. Even more profoundly, we can neglect to say "thank you" to God.

It is convenient to assume that we have somehow earned our gifts and that we are indeed "self-made." Misfortune is somebody else's fault or perhaps even an affliction from God—how could God do this to me?—but good things are only what we deserve. It is easier to ask for things, complain about things, or even fill God in on the news, while seeing the good gifts in our lives as our own doing, "good luck," or something to be taken for granted. True, we may remember to thank God for special blessings such as recovery from major illness or a narrow escape from disaster, but for many of us giving thanks for the everyday gifts is not a habit.

Like our prayers of adoration, prayers of thanksgiving remind us of the immensity of our debt and our utter nothingness without God's gifts. Our liturgical prayers of thanksgiving express this eloquently, but in language that is remote from the ordinariness of our lives. I find that I say the words mechanically, cognizant of their truth but rarely making the connection with the small blessings that punctuate my everydayness. The words are too grand, and perhaps there are too many of them for us to take them in. By contrast, in the spontaneous thanksgivings invited in the Prayers of the People, there are not enough words. While there is no shortage of response when the officiant bids prayers "for the special needs and concerns of this congregation," the sentence "We thank you, Lord, for all the blessings of this life" is most commonly met with a deafening silence.

It is an interesting exercise to close each day reflecting on occasions for thanksgiving, to name five or ten things for which we are grateful. I remember doing this rather self-consciously each Thanksgiving Day as a small child in Sunday school. We were a competitive bunch, and most of our thanksgivings were generalized pieties designed to impress the teacher. In our prayers of thanksgiving it is important to be specific and candid. Nothing is too big or too small not to be overlooked: I am grateful that I have received a huge salary increase, that my child has recovered from chicken pox, that a boring committee meeting has been canceled, and that my headache is gone. I am grateful for the feel of clean water in the shower. I am grateful that my colleague and I have forgiven each other so that, even if we are not exactly friends, we are no longer enemies.

We can bring playfulness to our thanksgivings and let ourselves enjoy the surprises that an increased awareness of God's goodness can bring. Instead of waiting until the end of the day, we can follow the example of our Jewish brothers and sisters and give thanks for small gifts as we encounter them, not being reluctant to include tiny or unlikely blessings. Somewhere I read that the writer G. K. Chesterton said grace over books before he began to read. We can give thanks for the goodness of a cup of tea, for the wonder of familiar words that suddenly leap from the page with new meaning, even for the all-embracing, all-forgiving friendliness of our big silly dog.

∽ Confession

In a way, confession is the opposite side of the coin from thanksgiving, for we are acknowledging our limitation and sinfulness over against God's perfection. I regret that the 1979 *Book of Common Prayer* has deleted an important sentence from the General Confession: "There is no health in us." To be sure, the words can sound like hypocritical groveling or abject defeat, but without God's love, there is no health in *us*. We cannot achieve it by ourselves. Many of us are uncomfortable with the confession of sin because it suggests that we might have some wrongdoing to confess and are therefore less than perfect, and that—horrors!—we might have the temerity to own up to it. Or we fear that acknowledging our imperfections honestly to other people, and even to ourselves, would fill us with despair.

The Book of Common Prayer includes moving prayers of confession to be said together in communal worship. They are powerful prayers, but it is possible to repeat them Sunday after Sunday without digging beneath the surface of beautiful words. If our confessions are to have any real effect on our spiritual lives it is important that they be clear and that we be unflinchingly aware of ourselves and our sinful ways of being. Specificity is essential. "I was unkind to my child" might mean that I finally raised my voice after being provoked by a manipulative adolescent who was more than a match for me, or it might mean that I struck my baby when her crying annoyed me. "I was untruthful" might mean that I spared someone's feelings by telling less than the truth—"Yes, that really is a becoming hair-cut"—or it might mean that we have committed adultery, perjury, or embezzlement. When we make our confession, whether it be in the words of the general confession in the context of worship, in the presence of a priest in the sacrament of reconciliation, or in our own solitary time of reflection, honesty and specificity are crucial. This is no time to imitate our political and military leaders who, when confronted with malfeasance, corruption, or mismanagement, respond blandly, "Mistakes were made." The passive voice has no place in prayers of confession.

It is also important to look for patterns. Our specific sinful actions, like the symptoms of an illness, are useful for identifying sinful ways of being. My throat is scratchy and my nose is running—aha! I have a cold! I tucked a motel towel into my suitcase, failed to call the supermarket cashier's attention to an error (in my favor), and made a few personal long-distance calls from the office—aha! I have stolen! It hurts to put hard names on what seem like "little" sins. Yet that is what confession is about: looking at ourselves with clear eyes, not groveling or condemning, but wholly honest. I find myself wishing that my sins were more interesting. The most exciting part of Milton's *Paradise Lost* is Lucifer's fall from heaven. Our sins are rarely Miltonic; rather, they are small, tacky, and shabby, which is somehow more embarrassing than if they were spectacular. But they are sins nonetheless.

It helps to have a spiritual director or a confessor whom we visit regularly and who can help us see ourselves more clearly. We have a tendency to confess the wrong sins, to be aware of small ones that are scarcely more than peccadillos even as we conveniently overlook our most hurtful short-comings. We fail to see the connection between apparently unrelated actions. We confuse guilt and shame. Guilt derives from our sinful actions or omissions; we are responsible, and our discomfort is salutary. On the other hand, shame—while sometimes even more painful than guilt—may result from circumstances beyond our control as well as from our own behavior. This is apparent to me from my work with survivors of abuse, who tend to blame themselves for their own suffering and need patient help in picking apart the strands of guilt and shame.

In solitary prayer or in preparation for sacramental confession, it is good to begin by reading the story of the prodigal son in Luke's gospel (15:11-32), then to ask, "In what way am I no longer worthy to be called God's son or daughter?" In prayers of confession, the main point is not how appallingly sinful *we* are, but rather how prodigally loving *God* is. It is important to let go of sins once they are confessed, even though it is tempting to hold on to them and carry them around because we are proud of them, feeling that they bestow a certain distinction upon us—just as hypochondriacs resist health. Goodness is not interesting; sin makes us *special*. Marlowe's Faust was damned not for his sinful actions, but because he pridefully regarded himself as so great a sinner as to be beyond redemption.

❧ Intercession

Prayers of intercession move us beyond ourselves into community. Mistakenly, we tend to group intercession with petition, but in intercession we are not really asking

God for anything. Pushed back to its Latin roots *(inter-cedere)*, the word simply means "to stand between" or "to stand in the midst." When we intercede, whether in prayer or in everyday life, we place ourselves before authority on behalf of another. It is no surprise that Mary has been invoked as intercessor over the centuries; what mother has not, perhaps wrongheadedly and irrationally, interceded on behalf of her child with an irate father, an exasperated classroom teacher, or the parole board of the state prison? Mary and her kindly (and apocryphal) mother Anne can be counted on to intercede for the least worthy among us.

Since we are all made in the image of God, united in our sinfulness and our glory, intercession is a democratic kind of prayer: we can all intercede for one another. We can name before God those in any need or trouble, known to us or unknown. This is the prayer of the family of believers, praying *through* Christ *in* the company of the faithful.

We intercede publicly in the liturgy, where the Prayers of the People are like a great net of intercession, taking in the universal church, secular authorities, the welfare of the world as well as the concerns of the local community, those who suffer and are in trouble, and the departed. Unfortunately, many times these prayers seem perfunctory and rushed, tucked in between the creed and the eucharist, as if we were in a hurry to get on with the *real* business at hand. They merit thoughtfulness and space for silence as well as the opportunity for additional brief prayers from the congregation. Led by a lay person standing in the midst of the congregation, they draw us together and remind us that we are knit together in a community much larger than our families or our parish. They prepare us for the meal that is to come.

Intercession is often the most vital part of our solitary prayer, perhaps because we turn to it when we feel most helpless or anxious. I cannot stop a friend's metastisizing cancer, but I can at least name him in my prayers. I cannot undo the destruction caused by a hurricane, but I can remember those made homeless in my prayers. I cannot ease the tensions between Arab and Israeli, but I can breathe a prayer for the troubled Holy Land.

We usually begin by praying for those with whom we live and work—family, friends, and colleagues—for they are the people closest to our hearts. It is important then to broaden the circle and to pray for those whom we do not know and will most probably never see. We can use the same categories as the Prayers of the People, but in our solitary prayer there is room for spontaneity. The strong sense of another's distress or the urgency of a situation may lead us to a narrower focus, leaving the other worthy "categories" for another time. Prayer, after all, is not something to be got through mechanically as we check off items on a list. Intercession lends itself to odd times and odd places: we can pray for others whenever and wherever the spirit comes upon us. I make a point of praying—just naming the person before God—when someone pops unexpectedly into my thoughts. Sometimes I follow up with a note or phone call, especially when the impression is strong and will not go away.

When we pray our intercessions, we are not bargaining with God, nor are we engaged in magical thinking. It is important to remember that we cannot pray people well, even though we all know situations where the effects of intercession have been palpable. At the same time, we all know situations where the most fervent prayers seemed to go unheard or were answered in a way that we cannot understand. It is cheap comfort to pretend that any amount of prayer can magically make everything all right, bring swift comfort to the grieving, and ease the pain of the suffering. It is excruciating to watch at the foot of the cross, yet if we live long enough and let ourselves experience life fully, we will find ourselves at some point in that desolate place. If nothing else, intercession holds the sufferer in the embrace of the community. The suffering is not lessened, but it is more bearable when one does not watch alone.

If we are brave, we will also pray for those whom we have hurt and for those who wish to hurt us. This can be hard, and we may feel like hypocrites, especially if we harbor bitterness and ill-will toward the person. It is enough just to name the person, to hold her briefly before God in our mind. If we can do this, we have taken a great step toward reconciliation and wholeness.

Sometimes it takes courage to ask for the prayers of others. When I hit a bad patch recently, I knew that I needed the prayers of my good friend Andrew (who prays for me regularly even in good times), but I found myself hesitating, picking up the phone and then putting it down, and—when I finally made the call—hoping that I could leave a message on the answering machine. Maybe, I told myself, I was just being dramatic—surely there were others who needed his prayers more! To ask for another's prayers is to admit helplessness and fear. It is to acknowledge that, no matter how "together" we might appear, we just cannot go it alone. We need God's help, and we need God's help mediated by the prayers of our friends.

If we are known as people of faith, we will be asked for our prayers not only by our fellow parishioners but by all sorts and conditions of people. Religious habits and clerical collars are dead giveaways, but a cross on a chain or a pin is sufficient to identify the potential intercessor. I have been asked for prayers on planes, in the subway, and in railroad stations. Once in a taxi the driver, a quintessentially tough New York cabbie, asked me for numbers to play the lottery.

I am not sure that this was precisely a request for prayer, but I offered him the dates of my two ordinations (not telling him, of course, the significance of the numbers). He might have experienced a conversion if the numbers turned out to be lucky. Often, I suspect, the persons who ask for our prayers have fallen away, are unchurched and want to come home. Others are agnostics or even atheists who have somehow caught a glimpse of God's love and want more. In their minds, prayer may be all mixed up with magic, but they have glimpsed its power. Who knows where that first step of asking for prayer will take them?

It is easy to agree to pray for someone and much harder to honor that pledge. Yet the promise of intercession is a serious commitment. It might help to keep a list, being sure to review it regularly. Unweeded lists can become unwieldy and turn intercession into a dreary chore.

Praying for others is not a means of making ourselves feel better. If we are praying from the depths of our soul, we cannot remain untouched. Because ultimately we cannot accomplish anything by our prayers, intercession is a small experience of watching at the foot of the cross. We grow in awareness of the suffering of others. We grow in awareness of our own complicity and power to hurt. We grow in awareness of the need to support our prayer with action. Serious intercession leads inevitably to an increase in generosity and an acute awareness of injustice.

ᔕ Petition

Petition, entreating on our own behalf, is the most common kind of prayer, the form that comes most easily and unbidden. At the same time, it is the prayer we feel most guilty about. Surely it is selfish to bother God by asking for gifts for ourselves when there are others who might need them more!

Small children are utterly uninhibited about asking, indeed begging and whining, for all manner of things—just watch the harried parent by the candy rack at the supermarket checkout or borrow a four-year-old and take a walk through Toys R Us. By the time we reach adulthood, though, most of us are socialized not to ask for anything. Little girls learn early that they are to think of others before themselves, while most boys are socialized to be independent and not to need anything from anyone. This early training does not mean we cease to yearn to possess all manner of treasure and trash, but our hankering is driven underground. We might become devious and manipulative, adept at getting what we want by indirection. Or we might just give up and grow accustomed to feeling deprived.

I recall my mother at the dinner table in my childhood. "Daddy, do you want more potatoes?" My father would politely decline. "Margaret, maybe Grandpa cares for some more potatoes." Before I could pass the serving dish, Grandpa also declined. "Well then," she would say, "I guess I'll have some myself." The dish would be duly passed. It is funny and a little poignant to look back sixty years at that scene around the big oak table. It was not always potatoes; sometimes it was pickled peaches, sometimes iced tea, and sometimes fried chicken. But I remember thinking with some irritation, "Why can't she just *ask* somebody to pass the potatoes?" She could not ask, of course. She saw her work as taking care of other people, feeding them literally and figuratively. She was not supposed to want anything for herself, even a humble potato. She waited for others to figure it out, disguising her own wishes and hoping that the others around the table would crack the code. They never did.

Similarly, we can become socialized to feel that petition is self-indulgent and greedy. This judgment can lead us to suppress our true selves in prayer, hanging back and hoping that God will crack the code and give us what we want. Yet scripture tells us that candid petition is a valid way of praying and that God does not expect to indulge in guessing games. The Lord's Prayer, for example, makes it clear that we are expected to ask for things, as a child would ask a beloved and trusted parent. Asking does not mean we get what we want at the time or in the form that we expect, if at all. But we are expected to ask. There are four petitions in that very short prayer Jesus taught his disciples to pray: for food; for forgiveness; to be spared trial and temptation; and to be delivered from evil. Clearly, Jesus expected his disciples to ask that their needs, both body and soul, be met.

In Luke's gospel, right after he has taught his friends the Our Father, Jesus tells an ironic story to drive home the point about candor in petition (11:5-13). "Suppose one of you has a friend," he begins, "and you go to him at midnight and say to him, 'Friend, lend me three loaves of bread.'" The friend tells you to go away because it is the middle of the night, but you keep pounding on the door so that finally he gets up and gives you what you want, just to get rid of you. "So I say to you, ask, and it will be given you; search, and you will find; knock, and the door will be opened for you," Jesus concludes. The message of the story seems to be, "Don't be afraid to ask, and keep at it!"

Of course, our petitions can be childish and self-serving—what I call the Bicycle Prayer: "Dear God, please let me find a bicycle under the Christmas tree." We all pray this way from time to time. At the end of a long day when I am in a hurry to get home, I catch myself peering down the subway tunnel at a distant light and muttering, "Dear God, let it be the C train." (More often than not, God sees fit to send a few E trains before answering my prayer.) We pray that we will find a convenient parking place or that our child will bring home a report card with all passing grades *for once*. We may attempt to bargain with God: "Just let me survive this crisis and I promise that I will...."

It can be a profitable exercise to try to discern what we *truly* want and need, and then to ask for it. Some version of the story of the magical three wishes appears in folk literature from all corners of the world: given the gift of three wishes, the wisher wastes or misuses all of them and ends precisely as poor as he was before. Thank God, we are not limited to three wishes! Thank God, the practice of prayer is not a guessing game!

To define our wants and needs is a similar exercise to ordering our loves. An old friend, director of a major zoo, once told me that, given the choice, the animals in his care preferred junk food to their optimum natural diet. "They'll take the Twinkie any day," he said. I think about those monkeys, spurning fresh fruit and reaching for a cupcake, when I try to work out what I truly want. I pray that I will be able to distinguish between spiritual Twinkies and real food, and to persevere in asking for that real food, not to hide behind the prayer of passivity: "Whatever you think, God. You know best. Whatever." I am invited—indeed expected—to pound on the door and ask.

Ultimately, though, our prayers of petition must be humble, rooted in our finitude. We will not always know our needs, or know what is truly best for us or for others. Jesus' prayer in the garden is our guide: "Father, if you are willing, remove this cup from me; yet, not my will but yours be done" (Luke 22:42). This is a hard prayer; please God, we will be able to pray it.

Chapter Four

Prayer Through the Centuries

From the Jesus Prayer to Lectio Divina

B eyond the basic categories of prayer we looked at in
chapter three—adoration, thanksgiving, confession,
intercession, and petition—there are many other ways of
praying. Our conversation with God is much too dynamic,
vital, and personal an undertaking to be shoehorned into a
neat schema, and we are right to be wary of those who
would reduce prayer to a recipe or insist that there is *one*
correct way of making ourselves open to God. The variety
and number of books and courses on particular "methods"
of prayer—Ignatian prayer, centering prayer, *lectio divina*,
praying with mantras (especially the Jesus Prayer), and
praying the rosary—belie such a limited approach.

In fact, the resources for prayer are so rich they can
threaten to overwhelm us, especially if we are tempted to
try everything at once. I have found that certain approaches fit better with some personalities than with others, and there are times in our lives when one method of
prayer will be more helpful than another. The way we
choose to pray is not as important as where it leads us: the
point is to focus on being open to God and not to make an

idol of the method. Any method can lead us into conversation with God.

In this chapter we will look at a number of different methods of prayer that Christians have found helpful over the centuries, as well as a few I have identified through my own experiences of prayer and spiritual direction.

∾ Ignatian Prayer

At the heart of Ignatian prayer is the conviction that God can be found in all things. As a consequence, this method appeals to our senses and encourages our imaginations. The gospel becomes vivid and alive as we put ourselves in the story. This can be a dynamic experience for anyone who has plodded through scripture, conscientiously squelching each stirring of fantasy. After all, the Bible is a holy book, isn't it? We are supposed to read it reverently, quieting our random thoughts and ignoring the pictures that flit through our minds, aren't we? If we let ourselves be guided by Ignatius of Loyola, a priest who lived in the sixteenth century and the founder of the Society of Jesus (better known as the Jesuits), the answer is a resounding *No!* In his spiritual exercises Ignatius invites us to read scripture as if we were there in person. We use all five senses to let ourselves see, hear, taste, and smell the events and places and people in the story. Mere reading is transformed into a lively, imaginative experience.

His spiritual exercises are currently enjoying renewed popularity, and not merely among Roman Catholics or clergy and members of religious orders. Ordinary folk of all denominations are discovering them, either in the intense experience of the traditional thirty day retreat or—more commonly—in the simpler way set forth in an annotation to the *Exercises:* "One who is educated or talented, but engaged in public affairs or necessary business, should take an hour and a half daily for the spiritual exercises." In either event, the exercises are undertaken under the guidance of a spiritual director skilled in Ignatian spirituality.

It is not necessary, however, to do all the spiritual exercises to benefit from Ignatius' approach to prayer. Welcoming the use of our imagination in prayer and the reading of scripture, instead of regarding it as a distraction, gives permission to those parts of ourselves that we often suppress in worship and brings an immediacy to our prayer. Only when we experience the gospel in the present tense can we truly own it. Instead of suppressing our five senses, we use them as a passageway into the mysteries of Christ's life. The gospels, after all, depict Jesus as a person who used and delighted in the senses. His denigrators—in the colorful language of the King James translation—called him "a gluttonous man, and a winebibber" (Luke 7:34). He told stories that abound in imagery of touch, taste, sight, hearing. He touched people when he healed them; he took his disciples' dusty feet in his hands and washed them. People brought their children to him so that he could touch them and bless them.

Hence gospel stories are especially good material for this type of imaginative meditation broadly called Ignatian. We read or hear a familiar story, then let ourselves be in that story and let the story be in us. In a sense this is a playful kind of prayer, for we give our imagination freedom to lead us where it will. Sometimes it takes us to surprising places where we hear surprising things.

ᕰ Centering Prayer

Like Ignatian prayer, centering prayer has moved into the spiritual mainstream in recent years. The popularity of transcendental meditation and other forms of eastern meditation in the 1970s and 1980s led eventually to a new awareness of similar resources in our own tradition. It has come as a surprise to many that silent, contemplative prayer has been practiced by Christians all along. New translations of *The Cloud of Unknowing*, a classic text on contemplative prayer written by an unknown author in the fourteenth century, are enjoying renewed popularity. Although the words "centering prayer" do not appear in the text—Thomas Merton is credited with supplying the twentieth-century name for this ancient way of praying—the very human and readable *Cloud* is the basic text for Christian contemplative prayer. The Cistercian writers Basil Pennington and Thomas Keating have made its teachings current and accessible in their books and workshops.

Much of the literature of the tradition, dating back at least to the writings of Evagrius of Pontus in the fourth century, proposes that there are stages and gradations of prayer, suggesting that some kinds are "better" or more advanced than others. They also intimate that contemplative prayer is the realm of "the arrived"—the proficient, if not the perfect. Hence dogged reliance on the classics can be discouraging and off-putting: this is not for me, this is for a holy somebody who lives in a Romanesque abbey without central heating and who makes a full-time work of prayer. I am convinced, however, that our temperament as well as our spiritual proficiency very much influences how we pray, so that wordless or imageless contemplation may not come easily to the sensate, highly imaginative person, whose prayers are nevertheless deep and valid. On the other hand, there are those who are drawn naturally to inner silence and sink gratefully into it.

Yet centering prayer is or should be accessible to all, in one form or another. Even the most imaginative among us has a need for focused silence in prayer. It is a challenge to seek stillness in our noisy and hectic world; I find it easier to quiet my thoughts and surrender to silence when I do it with others. This lessens the temptation to peek at the clock, cut the session short, or go off on mental tangents. Distractions beckon and can be better resisted when one is not alone. Shared silence is definitely more than the sum of its parts.

But what does one *do* in the silence? Centering prayer is deceptively simple: we quiet ourselves, perhaps stretch a bit to relax, find a comfortable posture with back straight and feet on the floor, close our eyes, and then begin to re- peat—silently—the prayer word we have chosen. It might be "love," "Jesus," or "Come, Lord." We match the word to our breathing, notice distractions when they appear, and then let them go. Distractions will come, at least for begin- ners. I find myself tempted by flashes of insight, positive and negative, or bright ideas for writing projects. Maybe I should suspend the prayer for a minute while I jot down a few notes, just a reminder so that not a word or thought gets lost? The internal monitor also intrudes, checking on my progress. It is sometimes self-congratulatory but more often disapproving: this is at best a B– prayer; surely you can do better than *this!* The prayer word is a kind of "white noise," intended to minimize these intrusions and keep us focused. When the prayer time has elapsed (ten minutes is good for beginners, but the time can be increased with practice), we gently emerge from the prayer.

The essence of centering prayer is its simplicity. A com- mon reaction to the first experience is a puzzled question: is that all? How do I know that I got it right? And what is *it*, anyway? Centering prayer is effortless—or should be. Ironically, doing nothing is often more of a challenge than simply being present and attentive. The anonymous author of *The Cloud of Unknowing* briskly commands a gen- tle passivity: "Wait with gracious and modest courtesy for the Lord's initiative and do not impatiently snatch at grace like a greedy greyhound suffering from starvation."[1] The point of it all is simply being there with God, going to God without any expectations. Childlike, we stop struggling and let ourselves rest, as the psalmist described:

But I still my soul and make it quiet,
    like a child upon its mother's breast;
my soul is quieted within me. (Psalm 131:3)

Centering causes us to leave time, space, and our own separateness behind. We are not seeking God so much as seeking our true selves, being who we really are. Yet centering prayer is by no means an exercise in self-centered introspection; rather, the experience of going to our own center leads us—as Thomas Merton observed—to the center of God. Open to our deepest self, we become open to our neighbor as well. We become aware of our own alienation and fearfulness, for identity based on differentiation makes us fearful: we are afraid of one another and the Other. But when we pass through our center to God's center we grow in compassion, which is the fruit of centering prayer. This is a glorious promise, as Merton writes in *New Seeds of Contemplation*: "When you and I become what we are really meant to be, we will discover not only that we love one another perfectly, but that we are both living in Christ and Christ in us and we are all one Christ. We will see that it is he who loves in us."[2] Similarly, six hundred years before Merton the author of *The Cloud of Unknowing* observed, "Now just as contemplative love nurtures perfect humility,

1. *The Cloud of Unknowing*, ed. William Johnston (Garden City, N. Y.: Doubleday, 1973), 36.
2. Thomas Merton, *New Seeds of Contemplation* (New York: Norton, 1972), 65.

so it is creative of practical goodness, especially charity. For in real charity one loves God for himself alone above every created thing and he loves his fellow man because it is God's law." Hence one who prays contemplatively knows no strangers and no enemies. Rather, "through contemplation he is so growing in practical goodness and love that, when he speaks or prays with his fellow Christians at other times [other than prayer time], the warmth of his love reaches out to them all, friend, enemy, stranger, and kin alike."[3]

When we let ourselves experience compassion, we cannot avoid suffering. Centering prayer is not an escapist way of closing the world out. Rather, by entering the deep silence, we let the world in.

ᔍ Lectio Divina

Lectio divina—holy reading—is a gift from the Benedictine-Cistercian tradition, beginning with the early days of western monasticism in the sixth century. Like centering prayer, it is deceptively simple, and its aim is movement toward God by resting, beyond words, in God's presence.

For most of us, reading is an intellectual undertaking: we read to gather information, to develop rational and logical constructs, to understand with our minds. There is subtle and not so subtle pressure in our educational systems and in society as a whole to read as much and as rapidly as possible. Even when we are reading for pleasure, we go for quantity and speed. I am amazed and a little embarrassed by my tendency to gulp down books as if they were mental fast food rather than an intellectual or spiritual gourmet meal. For me the sin of gluttony asserts itself not at the dinner table, but when I walk into one of the giant

---

3. *Cloud*, 80-81.

bookstores that dot the city. I want to read them *all* and, if possible, to own them *all*. My study has books in bona fide bookcases, books in shaky, makeshift constructions, and books stacked on the floor. And they are never quite enough.

To pray through holy reading, however, only one book is needed: the Bible. Instead of galloping over the text and ranging far and wide, *lectio divina* invites us to slow down and go deep. We begin with a passage of scripture—perhaps a favorite psalm, a gospel story, or a portion of the Sunday lectionary—reading slowly and thoughtfully. This is not a time to look things up in a commentary or ponder theological minutiae. Just read. It may be necessary to go over the passage a second time until a word, a phrase, or a sentence seems to leap from the page and engages our attention. This is the first step: reading. *Lectio.*

The next step is reflection on the words that have spoken to us: *meditatio.* Suppose the passage chosen is the familiar one from John's gospel in which Jesus tells his disciples, "In my Father's house there are many dwelling places" (John 14:1-6). Jesus' promise, "I will come again and will take you to myself," catches our eye, seems suddenly new and powerful. How could we have read and heard these words so many times and not been struck by them? It is as if we are reading them for the first time. This is the time to reflect prayerfully on the words, to hear them as if they are addressed to us personally—indeed to ruminate on them. Remember how cows chew a mouthful of grass over and over—no speedy gulping and swallowing for them! So we chew on the text, pray it, and let it pray itself in us. What would it be like for Christ to come and take us to himself? Those with lively imaginations might picture a scene of homecoming, while the highly intuitive might simply stay with the words and let their truth soak in. This is the time to be with the words and let them work on and in us until our prayer—*oratio*—emerges.

This prayer is both simple and subtle, arising from an openness to God and a yearning for God. It moves away from words to a place beyond intellect and imagination. As Sister Thelma Hall says in her wise book on *lectio:* "The goal of prayer is not thoughts or concepts or knowledge *about* God, however sublime, but God himself as he *is*, mysteriously hidden in my deepest, true self."[4] Just as in centering prayer, the one who prays is led to surrender self and simply to *be* in the loving presence of God. This final stage is *contemplatio*, resting in that love.

It is my experience that this final stage is not reached easily and is certainly not reached every time. This is, however, no reason to dismiss *lectio* as a fruitful way of praying. Comfort with the method comes with practice, and even those who tarry in the beginning stages can enjoy new perspectives on scripture. When we let ourselves be open to a few words, unhurriedly and without expectation, surprises are inevitable. Was that word really there all along? Is this what it means, that Jesus will come and take me to himself? Somehow the promise has become real, etched on our spirit, known and understood at a depth beyond words. The words on the page do not matter anymore.

∾ The Jesus Prayer

Jesus' injunction to avoid repetition in our prayer—"When you are praying, do not heap up empty phrases as the Gentiles do; for they think that they will be heard because of their many words" (Matthew 6:7)—has made many wary

---

4. Thelma Hall, R. C., *Too Deep for Words: Rediscovering Lectio Divina* (Mahwah, N. J.: Paulist, 1988), 41.

of brief prayers repeated over and over. Yet prayer using a mantra has been an essential part of eastern Christianity for nearly fifteen hundred years. In recent decades the West has discovered—or recovered—this way of repetitive prayer as well, known variously as the Jesus Prayer or the prayer of the heart.

Like *lectio divina* and centering prayer, the prayer of the heart is deceptively simple. The words "Lord Jesus Christ, Son of God, have mercy on me, a sinner" are repeated over and over dozens, hundreds, or thousands of times. Sometimes the text is shortened by omitting "Son of God" or the last phrase, "a sinner." At the heart of the prayer is the *Kyrie* of the eucharistic liturgy: Lord, have mercy; Christ, have mercy; Lord, have mercy. Stripped to its barest, it is a single word, the invocation of the name of Jesus. The words of the Jesus Prayer echo the prayers of those who encountered Jesus in the gospel stories, such as the blind beggar Bartimaeus who cried: "Jesus, Son of David, have mercy on me!" (Mark 10:47). In Luke's gospel Jesus tells the parable of the Pharisee and the tax collector, in which the Pharisee prayed publicly and boastfully while "the tax collector, standing far off, would not even look up to heaven, but was beating his breast and saying, 'God, be merciful to me, a sinner!'" (Luke 18:9–14).

The Jesus Prayer is a complete prayer, containing adoration, petition, and confession in twelve short words. St. John Carpathos offered the comforting idea that after each petition for mercy God secretly answers, "Child, your sins are forgiven." The words are prayed in harmony with our breathing, so that God is "taken in" as the first clause coincides with inhalation. Sinfulness, indeed all that is not of God, is let go as the breath is exhaled.

Those who prayed the Jesus Prayer believed that those especially chosen would come to a vision of the Divine

Light—the dazzling light of the Mount of Transfiguration that reflects the uncreated energies of the Godhead. This is an important reminder even for eclectic dabblers: no matter how silent and inward this prayer might be, it is not private. True prayer always occurs in the community of the faithful, even when we pray in solitude. The Jesus Prayer is transformative. As the nineteenth-century holy man Serafim of Sarov observed, "Have peace in your heart and thousands around you will be saved." Pray the prayer of the heart, and the world will be changed.

Through the Jesus Prayer believers sought the "union of the mind with the heart" so that the prayer would become the prayer of the heart, as natural as breathing. The prescribed posture was to sit with head bowed and eyes fixed on the place of the heart. My own preference is to sit in a chair with my back straight, feet flat on the floor, and hands resting in my lap. The prayer also lends itself to walking, to repetitive manual labor—scrubbing floors or sawing wood—and lying in bed. This relaxed approach might offend some practitioners of the prayer, but I find the Jesus Prayer a comfortable companion in a variety of situations and postures.

A delightful introduction to the Jesus Prayer is *The Way of the Pilgrim*, by an anonymous writer in the nineteenth century. The pilgrim, a simple holy man, wanders through the Russian countryside, moving deeper into the prayer as he recites it ever more frequently: he begins with three thousand repetitions daily and works his way up to twelve thousand. The prayer fills his life and touches all whom he encounters.

I have no aspirations to the holiness of this pilgrim, but the Jesus Prayer has become a companion in my prayer life. I hope that by imprinting it on my subconscious it will be with me for the rest of my life, especially at the end, when other words will perhaps be lost to me. In the mean-time, it can turn insomnia into a fruitful experience, the desert of waiting into an oasis, and manual labor into a kind of playful prayer. When I cut wood for the little stove in my workroom in Jenkins Hollow, I size up the log by the number of Jesus Prayers it will require. Old, dry logs can be dispatched in five, while a tough piece of oak might de-mand thirty.

Needless to say, this is a good prayer in times of pain or stress. It beats novocaine—nowadays, lydocaine—at the dentist's office. It is also an excellent silencer when we are tempted to say too much too quickly. Like counting to ten, silently saying a few Jesus Prayers can stave off angry out-bursts or premature, indiscreet utterances. Just a touch of peace in the heart can work wonders.

✑ Books of Prayers

Our solitary prayer time can also be fed by the written prayers of others. Most obviously for Anglicans, *The Book of Common Prayer* is a valuable but frequently neglected re-source. While the daily offices—morning and evening prayer—are intended for corporate worship, they can pro-vide a prayerful framework for the ordinary days of ordi-nary people, whether we pray in a small informal group or alone at our desks or at the kitchen table. The daily read-ings and psalms are listed in the lectionary at the end of the prayer book, but special calendars available in religious bookstores make it easier to find the right place with a minimum of page-turning. In the course of a year, you will have traveled through many chapters of scripture and dis-covered favorite psalms. Sometimes my own reading of the offices is perfunctory, almost mechanical; at other times, I ruminate, and the words on the page lead me into the wordless prayer of contemplation. Sometimes they pique my intellectual curiosity and make me think. In all events, praying the morning and evening offices is a fruitful way of praying. Like brushing our teeth, it is a valuable daily habit to cultivate.

Compline and the noonday prayers also lend themselves to individual devotion. These are short offices, taking only a few minutes, although they can be extended if a significant period of silent reflection is included. Compline—the name means "complete"—is an excellent way to close the day, letting go of cares and asking God's protection for the night. The four offices are remnants of the monastic tradition of praying the hours, punctuating the day with reminders that all time belongs to God.

Of course, there are other resources besides the prayer book. *St. Augustine's Prayer Book*, first published by the Order of the Holy Cross in 1947, continues to be a bestseller in their monastery bookstore. It is literally a handy little book, fitting into a pocket or taking practically no space in an overpacked suitcase. The flavor of the prayers it offers is Anglo-Catholic, and the language reminiscent of the 1928 prayer book, which can be momentarily off-putting for those who have grown unaccustomed to "thees," "thous," and "vouchsafests." Yet with its wealth of traditional prayers it remains my book of choice for travel—and not just because it is so handy.

The variety and number of collections of prayers seems endless. There are the breviaries of religious orders: one of my favorites is *The Daily Office* of the Anglican Franciscans of England, a gift from an English soul friend. I have used it for five years and still not exhausted the trove of canticles and prayers that have not yet found their way across the Atlantic. The Roman Catholic Christian Brothers are producing the *Companions for the Journey* series, a rapidly growing selection of short, accessible books "praying with" a variety of saints. Even if they are not followed rigorously, they prime the pump when we are stuck and bored with our own prayer. Further, they help us to befriend some saints who might otherwise remain remote and unapproachable.

Valuable as they are, books of prayers should be used with caution. We can rely on them to the exclusion of our own inner voice, instead of finding in them an invitation to grow in spiritual self-confidence. Even more serious, we can equate their presence on our bookshelf with the work of prayer. I have to keep reminding myself that it is not enough just to own the book! It must be taken in hand, lived with, and prayed through.

We can also pray with hymns. Some hymn texts are superb poetry, while others reflect embarrassing lapses of literary taste. It really does not matter. If the hymn expresses our prayer, it can be a way of opening ourselves to God. Recently I participated in a renewal mission in a Roman Catholic parish. The theme was "stories of the Spirit," and my liaison person asked if I knew any good hymns about stories. I could not think of any in the Episcopal hymnal, but I recalled one from my Presbyterian childhood, searched among the books, and found it in my Baptist hymnal. It was a memorable experience to hear "Tell Me the Old, Old Story" sung, first hesitantly and then with growing vigor, in a South Boston Catholic church. Since then the hymn has embedded itself somewhere in my subconscious; I am not sure whether I am praying it or simply being haunted.

～ Informal Ways of Praying
Beyond these traditional ways of praying, I have found some informal categories of prayer of my own.

The Tevya Prayer

Prayer can be simply—and profoundly—conversation with God. I call this the Tevya Prayer, after the milkman protagonist in *Fiddler on the Roof.* Tevya was an observant Jew, but his true prayer was saved for times when he was alone in the barn with his old horse. Then he would talk to God, intimately and uninhibitedly. He would question, complain, and talk passionately about his hopes and disappointments. The Tevya Prayer is the polar opposite of our polite, carefully constructed prayers couched in appropriately "religious" language. It is spontaneous conversation, very much in the vernacular, between friends who hold nothing back from each other.

The danger in the Tevya Prayer is that it can turn into a one-sided newscast. If it is to be a true conversation, you must be willing to listen. The Lord says to the psalmist, "Be still and know that I am God." Sometimes in our prayer, just as in conversation with a friend, we need to unburden ourselves. We chatter on anxiously, repeating ourselves and not pausing for breath. We ask for counsel, then cannot be silent long enough to receive it. There is nothing wrong with talking ourselves out if then we are ready to listen. At times, it is the only way that we can empty ourselves and be ready to receive.

Most of us do not enjoy the solitude of a barn and the company of a sympathetic horse, but the Tevya Prayer lends itself well to walking and manual labor. Be prepared for curious looks if you engage in it on crowded city streets. Be prepared, too, for family members to question your mental stability when they hear animated conversation from the kitchen.

The Panic Prayer

Sometimes we forget all about God until we find ourselves in a bind, and then we want to get through immediately. Even nonbelievers pray some version of this prayer: Just let me pass this exam or live through this operation or find a new job, and I promise that.... Here follows some version of "I will never sin again."

When I worked as a hospital chaplain, I regularly encountered the Panic Prayer on visits to patients about to undergo surgery. I remember particularly a burly truck driver who was facing a coronary bypass in the morning. "Chaplain," he said, "if I pull through, I'm going to clean up my act. I'll never use salt again, and I'll never miss Sunday church again." I think I startled him when I responded, "Do you really think God keeps track of your church attendance? The change in diet seems like a good idea, and I'm all for worshiping regularly, but I can't envision a *loving* God who would be swayed by your promise of perfect attendance." It turned out to be a good visit. Joe talked about how scared he was, and I agreed that I would be scared too. We talked a little more about God, the God who made us and wants us to be whole. I promised to pray for him and then to check in with him after the surgery. That was ten years ago. I think of him now and then and wonder about his church attendance. I have a feeling that it is still far from perfect.

I always feel a little cheap after I have indulged in a Panic Prayer, but I know that even if it is rather childish—childish and grabby, not childlike and trusting—it is still prayer. If we forget all about our anguished entreaty once the crisis is past, we will remain in an immature and self-centered place. If, on the other hand, we are paying as much attention to our own prayer as we expect from God, the Panic Prayer can be an occasion of thanksgiving and new insight.

We can begin to grow up to a new understanding: that we do not make deals with a Scorekeeper God. We might even understand that God is more than a scorekeeper.

Praying in the Cracks

Perhaps this reflects my midwestern upbringing, but I hate to waste anything. There are so many empty spaces in an ordinary day, seemingly useless times when there is nothing to *do*, when we feel trapped in passivity. While the dentist is drilling. While we wait for the kettle to boil. While we watch the plastic bag fill slowly with platelets at the blood bank. While we wait in line at the toll booth. While we sit in a dark subway tunnel, held in a "momentary delay." While we hear for the third time the soothing canned message, "Thank you for holding. Your call is important to us."

There are so many cracks in the day that can be filled with prayer. These might be prayers of intercession. We can carry a sick or dying friend with us through the day, gently letting the prayer lie just below the surface of our consciousness, ready to emerge in the "empty" moments. Our daily prayer in the cracks might be triggered by the morning news report of conflict, catastrophe, and suffering. The big story this morning is a plane crash. I will let those people be with me today—the travelers who died, the few who survived, their families who are flying to the scene, the rescue teams sifting through the wreckage. They will fill the cracks today.

On the other hand, prayer in the empty spaces need have no specific focus. This can be a time for simple, repetitive prayer, such as the Jesus Prayer. Repeated over and over, simple prayers can sanctify seemingly unholy times and places. I have recommended the practice to friends who are frightened of flying; it can help even as they grip the arm rest white-knuckled and choose their funeral hymns. I use it myself at the dentist's, the scene of ultimate helplessness. It somehow gives meaning to the moments of passivity and discomfort. After one bout of extensive work, Herb, my dentist, commented, "I'm not always sure where you are or what's going on with you." I should have told him; it was an opportunity for witness, from a good Episcopalian to a good Methodist, but I did not. He probably thought it was some New Age thing.

Praying in the cracks leads us to prayer in unlikely places. There is something gloriously symbolic about praying in the shower and something deeply poignant about praying on a dirty, sinister-feeling city street. I have prayed watching the first red line of dawn from an airplane window, and I have prayed in airports and train stations, places that are anonymous nonplaces, impermanent and interchangeable. I have prayed walking down deserted country roads, and I have prayed in supermarkets. The practice of prayer in unlikely places is a powerful reminder that God can be encountered anywhere.

Praying with Our Hands

Like Thomas, who wanted to touch the wounds of the resurrected Jesus, many of us are tactile beings for whom words are not enough. Valuing the evidence of our senses, we yearn to touch and feel as we pray. Using our hands can help us be centered in prayer. It must be a sign of God's gracious irony that Protestants are now discovering the rosary, while many Roman Catholics regard it as a pre-Vatican II relic, beloved of older women in ethnic neighborhoods.

The rosary lends itself to many prayers, not just the traditional mysteries. We can use it for intercessions, naming a name and seeing a face as each bead slips through our fingers. We can use it as the Orthodox use their knotted prayer ropes, saying a Jesus Prayer with each bead. Or we can create our own categories for the decades—the groups of ten beads, separated by a single "Our Father" bead—as I did for my own prayer time a few years ago. Some of the categories were obvious. One decade for my loved ones, another for the sick and suffering. The decade for prisoners helped me remember prisoners of conscience, those unjustly imprisoned, political prisoners, those undergoing torture, prisoners on death row, those who probably belonged in prison but merited prayers nonetheless, and prisoners of addiction. I devoted another decade to victims: abused children, victims of domestic violence and sexual abuse, those killed in the Holocaust and in other "ethnic cleansings," those snatched from their homes and sold into slavery. The fifth decade was for those upon whose work and care I relied: farmers, truck drivers, physicians, store clerks, factory workers, migrant harvest workers—this was a long and variable list, but it was easy each night to find ten persons or groups, most of whom I would never see, to whom I was indebted. With each prayer, it was as if I held someone in my hand. Most of the prayers were intercessory, but there were also prayers of thanksgiving and confession.

Holding that little circle of wooden beads in my hands opened my eyes to broader vistas in solitary prayer. I was free to shift my focus as I grew in awareness or as circumstances demanded. Nothing about my homemade system was immutable, and I often found myself wondering what new categories would suggest themselves. It was an illuminating and humbling exercise to devote ten beads to my enemies and those who wished me harm.

We can also pray with our hands in almost any kind of rhythmic, repetitive work. Needlework can be a beadless rosary, with each stitch coinciding with a prayer. As I said earlier, I love to saw wood to the rhythm of the Jesus

Prayer. Scrubbing a floor (preferably on hands and knees) can be a time of vigorous, purgative prayer. Even repetitive computer or assembly line tasks can be occasions for prayer.

One of my artist friends prays with her hands, bypassing words completely. I am awed by her pictures and carvings. She deprecates her own talent and is a little uneasy, since working with her hands and eyes brings her such intense joy. Surely praying should be harder work! (My grandmother would agree: no medicine was efficacious unless it tasted vile.) Another friend, by no means an artist, nevertheless is able to draw her prayers in pastel chalks. They would not pass muster in an art class, but they are powerful and eloquent revelations of her ongoing conversation with God.

To pray with our hands expands our vision of prayer. It brings us in touch with God's created, tangible world, for it involves our bodies as well as our minds. It can refresh us when our prayer feels stuck and dry.

The Cosmic Complaint

This category needs little explanation, but I offer an example. On my kitchen wall there is a poster, now a little grimy and tattered. If I had known how much a part of my life it would become, I would have had it framed nearly twenty years ago when I received it as a going-away-to-seminary gift.

> A prayer to be said
> when the world has gotten you down
> and you feel rotten
> and you're too doggone tired to pray
> and you're in a big hurry

and besides you're mad at everybody—
Help!

Sometimes this is the only prayer possible.

Chapter Five

Practices of Prayer

Retreats and Journaling,
Sacramental Confession and Spiritual Direction

The closet in my grandmother's bedroom was deep and narrow. At the very back, along with a bottle of Four Roses bourbon (for medicinal purposes, as Grandma was officially a teetotaler) was an enormous old satchel filled with scraps of cloth. It was probably not nearly as big as I remember it, but to my child's eyes it appeared limitless, filled with fascinating bits that my grandmother turned into doll clothes, quilt squares, and patches when she was not engaged in some larger project. I loved the crazy variety of the scrap bag—bits of jewel-toned silk, practical cotton prints, strips of embroidery or lace, scraps of heavy tweed cut from an overcoat no longer fit to wear. There was a wild randomness to the collection, for the pieces seemed to have nothing to do with each other.

I have found myself thinking of Grandma's satchel as I approach the end of this first section on classic approaches to prayer. At this point I find myself with a satchel of scraps, assorted resources with seemingly little to do with one another but all linked with the practice of prayer. I invite you to rummage in the satchel, take what is helpful, and leave the rest.

❧ What Can I Expect on a Retreat?

Retreats are currently in fashion, not just for the markedly pious but for all sorts and conditions of men and women. In fact, we need to be cautious in our use of the word, which is increasingly applied to almost any activity away from parish or office: marathon off-site business or vestry meetings, parish-sponsored family outings, and trips to the beach or ski slopes for the youth group. Necessary or recreative as such events might be, they are not retreats in the traditional sense.

Put succinctly, a retreat is an intentional time away for prayer. This practice of retreating from the activities and tasks of the everyday in order to focus on prayer was modeled most fully by Jesus. Even a cursory reading of one of the gospels shows the rhythm of his life and ministry, a ministry of activity—preaching, teaching, healing, talking—alternating with times of going apart, either alone or with his disciples, for rest and renewal. Even when those around him are clamoring for healing, Jesus removes himself periodically. Sometimes they follow him; sometimes they are waiting when he returns. Most striking is his return from the Mount of Transfiguration: he comes immediately upon a scene of agitation, where the disciples have tried in vain to heal an epileptic boy, the scribes are arguing, and the crowd is surging. He has returned from solitude to engagement. The lesson here is clear: the retreat—for the experience of the transfiguration *was* a retreat, a time set apart for complete openness to God—comes in the midst of life with all its demands. "Real life," often with a vengeance, awaits us upon our return. But if we wait until everything is in order, until no one needs us, until there is "time," we will never follow Jesus' example and go apart.

Our prayerful openness to an encounter with God distinguishes a retreat from a vacation. There may be, of course, some overlapping, for a good retreat usually leaves the retreatant feeling better emotionally and physically as well as spiritually. But it may also leave us stirred up and uneasy, aware that a next step needs to be taken and that God is nudging us powerfully toward action.

An encounter with God cannot be programmed. The time apart might turn out to be "simply" that—a time of rest, prayer, and openness. We might arrive with the intent of spending an uninterrupted forty-eight hours on our knees on a cold chapel floor and find ourselves instead succumbing to the urge for a long nap or an inviting novel. Maybe we will stick with scripture and observe the regular monastic hours of prayer. No mountaintops, no angels singing, but a spiritually fruitful time nonetheless! On the other hand, the retreat might be a pivotal, even life-changing experience. The retreat time may be surprising or quite ordinary, but if we are open and humbly attentive it will never be merely a bland pious exercise without fruits.

We might ask: why go away? Can I not be attentive and open to God just as well in my office or my car or my kitchen? Isn't the idea of a retreat a little bit medieval, especially for busy people with crowded schedules? A good retreat offers us two special gifts: simplicity and silence. In our daily lives we are overwhelmed by stimuli of all kinds—visual, auditory, intellectual, aesthetic, and emotional. We are crowded by noises, sights, and things. On the other hand, the typical retreat space is stripped of nonessentials, offering privacy and austere sufficiency. It is easier to be open to God when we have separated ourselves, just for a little while, from material distractions.

The silence of a traditional retreat may cause us more apprehension than the stark simplicity of space. We wrap ourselves in sound because silence leaves us open and vulnerable. In the prayerful silence of a retreat, we are listening and receptive. Such prayerful silence is more than the absence of noise, more than refraining from the spoken word. It invites us to an inner stillness, active and creative, fully open to the encounter with God. It can be refreshing, disquieting, or a little of both. Especially at meals taken in silence new retreatants may feel awkward: how much eye contact is seemly when you are not talking? And isn't the crunch of that celery loud! With time, however, the stillness of the retreat becomes a comforting, familiar garment.

Typically, one makes a retreat at a convent or monastery. Diocesan and ecumenical conference centers are possible sites, but are usually designed for multipurpose activities, with a "one space fits all" approach. Rooms that are suitable for youth group outings and vestry conferences may not lend themselves to the contemplative experience. By contrast, there is something about a prayed-in space and a community comfortable with silence that makes the experience feel natural. All those hours and years of prayer have soaked into the walls. You may never know who has slept in the bed before you or who will sit in your seat in the chapel next, but there is a sense of connection and shared purpose.

At the Anglican Benedictine monastery where I feel most at home, guests are invited to say a prayer for the next occupant as they make up the bed before their departure. When I was there not long ago, I learned that a group would be coming that weekend from my old parish. I checked with the guestmaster to learn the name of the next occupant of my room. I had known Alyce nearly twenty years earlier as a fellow parishioner and was not at all sure that she would remember me. Nevertheless I wrote a little note, nothing serious, just a greeting and expression of pleasure that we were sharing a room. Months later, I happened to be in that parish, and a woman asked to speak with me for a moment. She identified herself as Alyce and said she wanted to talk about her October retreat. "I had a sense of your presence the whole time," she told me. I was a little uneasy and said, "I hope it was a friendly presence, at least."

"Oh yes," she replied, "it felt good, but I just couldn't understand it. Then when I was making up the bed for the next person, I had to pull it out from the wall a little bit, and there was your note on the floor. It must have fallen somehow. I hadn't seen it until then." We had been linked in the prayerful silence of a prayerful place. I didn't even try to understand it, but I know that it would never have happened in a Holiday Inn!

Most religious houses, Roman Catholic as well as Anglican, welcome retreatants, but the prospect may be daunting to the beginner. I recall my first visit to a convent where I later came to feel very much at home. I was sure that I would do something terribly wrong, set off alarm bells, and possibly be expelled as an infidel. The sisters seemed to genuflect at almost, but not quite, everything, and I was at a loss to figure out the pattern. Added to that was my worry that I might trespass on some sacred precinct. Since then, I have come to trust and appreciate the careful hospitality of religious houses. I know that as a visitor I do not have to figure everything out. Rather, I can let myself be welcomed and guided in the custom of the community.

Beginners may be more comfortable in a group, but one can go on retreat as an individual. A telephone call to the guest master/mistress ensures that space is available. A donation for room and meals is suggested, and special arrangements can usually be made in cases of hardship. Guests are normally welcome at community worship; a retreat is a wonderful opportunity to experience the monastic hours of prayer. Typically, retreats allow for a minimum of two nights away; a week is much better. But even in two days, a rhythm of alternating community and solitary prayer, meals and rest begins to establish itself. It is better to make a brief retreat than to forego the experience in the hope that ideal conditions for a more lengthy stay will somehow magically come about.

Recently my work took me to several Roman Catholic Benedictine houses in Oregon, Alabama, and Kansas over the course of six months. I felt I had stumbled onto a sacred hotel chain; despite external differences, the monasteries were remarkably the same. When I walked through the door, I immediately knew where I was and I knew that I was welcome. I felt the strong connection between the houses: these women were truly sisters even though they lived hundreds of miles apart. "Oh, yes," Sister Antoinette in Oregon would say, "Sister Maurus is an old friend." And Sister Maurus in Alabama would tell me stories about her trip to Russia with Sister Johnette from Kansas. In each house, they expanded the circle to let me in for a little while, to share good conversation, prayers, and stillness. I knew that whenever I might return it would be a homecoming.

While it is possible to make a retreat as an individual and simply to spend unstructured time in re-creation, most religious houses also offer a program of scheduled retreats throughout the year. Some are seasonal: every retreat conductor knows that Advent and Lent are the busy seasons for scheduled retreats. Others are thematic: retreats for singles, married couples, caregivers to the terminally ill, the bereaved, the recovering addicted. Still others might combine opportunities for creativity with quiet reflection: these are retreats for journal writers, poets, and amateur painters.

The great figures in the Christian tradition—Julian of Norwich, Francis of Assisi, John of the Cross, Teresa of Avila, and a host of others—can also provide a focus for a retreat. Retreats called Benedictine Experiences offer retreatants the experience of living the Benedictine Rule for a week, combining work, study, and prayer in a monastic setting. Members of parishes may make retreats together; once established, the time away becomes an important part of community life, even when a relatively small number of people participate. Directed retreats are another possibility: the silent time is punctuated by daily meetings for spiritual direction by a member of the community. In short, there are all sorts and conditions of retreats. The common denominator is the intent: receptivity to the voice—or silence—of God. This means departure from routine activities to a simplified environment, where the retreatant is freed from demands and distractions.

~ Keeping a Journal

I once attended a journal workshop where my fellow participants arrived with bulging volumes the size of telephone books. "When do these people find time to live?" I wondered. The method being expounded was intricate and rigid. I was enriched by some of my learnings but left the weekend convinced that journaling—like prayer—should respect the individual. In fact, it is not helpful for everyone to keep a journal. A compulsive reader and writer myself, I have learned to rein myself in when talking with those who seek my counsel. For the dyslexic or simply for those who find writing a chore, the prospect of journaling is almost punitive, a burden rather than a path to new freedom. These folk might turn to wordless journaling: I have two friends, neither an artist, whose journals consist of pictures, sometimes roughly and inexpertly done but powerful nonetheless.

When I was a child, each Christmas I received a leatherbound diary, one lined page for each day of the year. I enjoyed the promise of the pristine little book, but soon found that promise turned to burden. Theoretically, one wrote something every day. I would fall behind, then in an industrious flurry fill in the empty pages: "Went to school today. Practiced the piano. We had meat loaf for supper. Not much happened." I did not permit myself the pleasure of fantasy or, for that matter, honesty. They would have been interesting little books if I had recorded my daydreams or the moods and tensions of my complex household: "I want to be a doctor when I grow up. I hate practicing the piano. Grandma hates Germans; she calls them Huns and says they kill babies." German was the first language of my gentle father Otto; I could not imagine him killing babies, but clearly Grandma had him or his dangerous relatives in mind.

A journal is a useless burden, even an affliction, if it is kept under compulsion and without candor. My compulsion was self-imposed: if I had been given the book, I was supposed to write in it. Regularly. No blank pages, even though our lives are punctuated with blank pages. Besides, it was no place for honesty. Well brought-up children wrote *nice* things. My lack of candor was also self-imposed (though no doubt prudent).

Honest journals are windows to the soul. Unselfconscious truth-telling about the details of everyday life and the writer's reaction to them is a powerful spiritual exercise. It is so tempting to make ourselves look good, even in our own eyes, and to disregard our frequently shabby motives. May Sarton's candid journals describing sickness and the increasing frailty of age, culminating in *Endgame:*

A Journal of the Seventy-Ninth Year, permit us to visit the innermost thoughts and feelings of a complex and creative woman grappling with the fundamental questions of life and death. Similarly, Henri Nouwen, in *The Genesee Diary: Report from a Trappist Monastery,* writes frankly of his self-centered anger:

> Today, I realized how, especially during work which I do not much like [he had been assigned to work in the monastery bakery], my mind starts feeding upon hostile feelings. I experience negative feelings toward the one who gives the orders, imagine that the people around me don't pay attention to my needs, and think that the work I am doing is not really necessary work but only there to give me something to do. The more my mind broods, the farther away from God and neighbor I move.[1]

No Brother Lawrence he! In his journal Nouwen admits that he feels slighted when he is not noticed or thanked. He is angry at the hard manual labor assigned to him—he worked with heavy stones when he was not in the bakery—and the apparent inefficiency of his monk-supervisor on the project. At first reading he seems rather spoiled, a spiritual dilettante, playing for seven months at being a monk and complaining inwardly all the way. But upon reflection I admired his directness. For all his well-established reputation as a writer and teacher on things of the Spirit, he was willing to let us see a limited and fallible human being. Maybe he was not so far from Brother Lawrence after all.

Anne Frank gave her journal a name—Kitty—and wrote as though she were talking to a trusted friend. Even now, more than fifty years after her death and especially as the

---

1. (Garden City, N.Y.: Doubleday, 1976), 29-30.

unexpurgated text becomes available, readers are gripped by the directness and clarity of her voice. She never attended a journal workshop, but she understood fully the vitality and intimacy of the written word. Her contemporary, Etty Hillesum, also recorded the spiritual struggle of her attraction to Christianity and the harsh reality of her life as a Dutch Jew. Bright and eccentric, Etty was a seeker who never quite fit in. Her voluminous journal is painfully straightforward. I find myself impatient with her, wanting her to be consistent, wanting her to realize the wrong choices she is making and, above all, wanting her to grasp the peril of her situation and save herself. Like Anne, she was eventually deported to a concentration camp, where she died.[2]

Recently, I came across another journal, the matter-of-fact recordings of the daily life of a woman who lived two hundred years ago. Martha Ballard, a midwife who lived in Maine in the early days of this nation, painstakingly wrote down the details of her professional and domestic life.[3] She would be surprised, I think, to hear her diary characterized as a spiritual document. She might well say, "I just wrote down what happened—babies delivered, people dying, housework done, garden tended." Yet her deep faith and equally deep compassion shine through every terse entry. Unlike Anne Frank, she did not give her journal a name, but it was clearly her best friend with whom she could be unabashedly herself. It was an avenue of freedom in a harsh, constricted life.

---

2. Etty Hillesum, *An Interrupted Life*, tr. Arno Pomerans (New York: Pantheon, 1983).

3. Martha Ballard, *A Midwife's Tale: The Life of Martha Ballard Based on Her Diary, 1785-1812*, ed. Laurel Thatcher Ulrich (New York: Vintage Books, 1990).

Whatever form it takes, the journal should be an instrument of liberation. It can be a means of reflection and self-examination; it can also be a way of prayer. I know people who write carefully in ink—fountain pen only, no ballpoints—in beautifully bound little books. Others fill spiral notebooks, the kind sold in college bookstores. For years I wrote my journal on the typewriter; now I have switched to the computer. A loose-leaf notebook allows for inclusion of poems, letters, even newspaper clippings—bits that belong in the journal even though they are not my words, chiefly because they are voices in my inner conversation. Some people write daily, some weekly, some when they feel a strong urge to self-expression. The form and the rhythm of writing is not important; nor is the content rigidly restricted to "the spiritual." The journal is an inner conversation, sometimes narrative and sometimes commentary, about anything of deep concern to the writer. It raises questions that cannot be answered, and it may evoke insights that startle the writer.

In the context of this book, the journal is in many ways a means of self-direction since the life of the writer is its raw material and increased self-knowledge is its goal. Implicit here, as in traditional spiritual direction, is the question, "Where is God in all this? How has the Holy Spirit been active in my life? What is the will of God for me?" This does not mean that we struggle to create a pious document, full of devout language. Rather, it should be an expression of our truest voice, straightforward and natural.

It is impossible to keep a journal honestly unless we feel safe. The book, in whatever form, must be secure from inquisitive eyes. It is a gross violation to read another's intimate thoughts, although the writer may occasionally wish to share some portion of an entry with a friend or spiritual director. I am convinced that fear of unwelcome intrusion keeps many from even attempting a journal. Heavily self-edited, the journal quickly loses its authenticity and the writing becomes an empty exercise. So finding a safe place is imperative, but even more important is assurance that members of the household understand the significance, indeed the sacredness of the ordinary-looking book or notebook. Some people discard old journals periodically so that others will not be injured should they someday learn of negative feelings they had not suspected, perhaps after the writer's death. This is probably prudent, but hard to do! The journal becomes a part of its author, with a life of its own.

So what to write? Like the psalms, the journal can give expression to our joys and fears, our love of God and our occasional anger at God, our trust and our despair. We can rewrite familiar prayers and psalms, or compose our own. We can write letters to God. If we are willing to surrender to our imagination, we can carry on a conversation with our favorite saints: my apocryphal friend St. Anne and I have had some wonderful visits. We can write poems and draw pictures even if we lack a shred of artistic ability. We can simply write about the events and feelings of our very ordinary lives, seen through the God-lens. Once we befriend our writing and lose our self-consciousness, the journal becomes a reliable and intimate companion. It accepts us as we are and invites us to ever deeper insight.

∾ Is Spiritual Direction for Me?

For many faithful churchgoers, "spiritual direction" is not a household word. The picture conjured up may be frightening, suggesting an unhealthy relinquishing of responsibility to a Rasputin-like guardian of the soul, a harsh and unloving figure of spiritual authority who will force us to our knees. Or there may be an aura of the medieval or monastic about the term—attractive, perhaps, but far removed from the complexity and chaos of our lives in the late twentieth century. Then too, we might think of spiritual direction as something desirable for the especially holy—clergy, perhaps, or seminarians and members of religious communities—but not for us. And yet many of us have experienced the need and hunger for spiritual direction, even though we may lack the vocabulary or the trust to identify our questions: Who are we in our relationship with God? How do we pray? How can we live out our professed beliefs? What do we do when we fall short?

These are the questions we bring to spiritual direction. The ministry is ancient and, until recently, much neglected. It has been rediscovered in part because of the Cursillo movement, but even more because of the failure of mainstream religion, the New Age movement, and psychotherapy to satisfy the profound but unarticulated yearning of the individual Christian for a deeper relationship with God. The tradition is there. It remains for us to build on it, and to work out a model of spiritual direction that is alive and meaningful for those in the "mixed life"—those who are psychologically aware, who are seekers, and who have no romantic illusions that they can or must be quasi-monastics as they cope with jobs, spouses, partners, children, taxes, and unpaid bills.

Spiritual direction defies precise definition because we are speaking of an art, not a science. Although there are valuable books on the subject and responsible training programs for those who possess the charism for this work, even experienced directors continually learn and grow in their understanding of what this rich ministry is all about. Similarly, those receiving direction find themselves moving to ever deeper levels of prayer and insight. In the absence of a precise definition, images and metaphors are helpful. The spiritual director is a midwife of the soul, present and attentive as new life emerges. The spiritual director offers hospitality, in the holy tradition of Abraham entertaining the angels. The spiritual director is a teacher, a rabbi, after the model of Jesus, who was called "Teacher" by those who loved him. But whether we call him teacher, midwife, or host, the spiritual director is always and above all a holy listener.

The holy listener does not engage in friendly chats or problem-solving sessions. Rather, the conversation of spiritual direction occurs in the presence of God. As the twelfth-century Cistercian spiritual director Aelred of Rievaux said, "Here we are, you and I, and I hope a third, Christ Jesus, is in our midst." The holy listener knows that the space between himself and the directee is sacred space, God-filled space. And he knows that he does not work alone.

So the spiritual director is able to put herself out of the way and thereby to be totally present to the person sitting opposite. Because she is disinterested (not at all the same as uninterested), she is able to listen critically but without judgment. She is able to ask hard questions, to sit comfortably with silence, not to be frightened by tears, and to rejoice in God's love. She is ready for whatever may come and immune to the temptation to "fix" anything. Above all, the spiritual director is humble and reverent, aware that she is being entrusted with another's very being.

Who are these holy listeners? Spiritual directors are men and women, lay, ordained, and members of religious communities. They may be highly trained in theology, or they may simply be people of prayer who walk closely with God. They are people of tested faith who have survived the peaks and valleys of the spiritual life—to say nothing of the arid plains and swamps.

Finding the right spiritual director may take time and effort. Chemistry is important: it is not easy to speak of one's life of prayer even to a warm and accepting listener. From my dentist or computer technician I hope for competence and integrity, but from my spiritual director I want loving detachment. In searching for a director I would begin by praying for guidance and awareness. Sometimes the right director is almost literally next door, but the seeker has not thought of him in these terms. The parish priest may know of a suitable director. Further, almost all religious houses offer spiritual direction. I usually suggest a visit, a short retreat if possible, just to get the feel of the community. Someone at the convent or monastery will be ready simply to talk about the possibility of spiritual direction.

When people come to me to initiate an exploratory conversation about spiritual direction, I try to find out what they are looking for in a director. What are they hoping to find? What brought them to me? How do they think I might be able to be helpful? Even when my schedule is full and I know that I must say "No," it is important to be welcoming and to let seekers know that you take them seriously. People are often reluctant to broach the subject, but it is an honor to be asked to serve as someone's spiritual director, even if the request must be denied.

What happens after one has established a relationship with a spiritual director? Director and directee meet regularly, usually for an hour once a month but sometimes at greater intervals. Confidentiality is inviolate: the director never repeats what she has heard. The meeting is implicitly prayerful, and usually there is spoken prayer as well as the intimacy of shared silence. Many people want to talk about prayer or to ask for help in finding a place for God in their busy lives. Others want to make sense of their lives—that is, to see their day-to-day struggles through the lens of their Christian commitment. Since there is a "God-component" in all our human experience, any matter of deep concern can provide the raw material for the direction session.

What are the fruits of spiritual direction? Most of us are so accustomed to being spiritual Lone Rangers that we are unaware of the burden we are carrying. To have the prayerful support of a trusted other who cares greatly about us but wants nothing from us can set us free to know ourselves better as we stretch and grow in our relationship with God.

~ The Sacrament of Reconciliation

"All can, some should, none must." I do not know who first articulated this succinct summary of the Anglican approach to confession, but it states our position adequately. The 1979 *Book of Common Prayer*, however, has brought a new awareness of this sacramental rite that has often been regarded as the province of Anglo-Catholics and Roman Catholics, and as mildly suspect by the ordinary person in the pew. The very words "auricular confession" are formidable, suggesting something arcane and maybe even a little dangerous. Yet the possibility of making one's confession as an individual, with infinitely greater specificity than is possible in the General Confession of the liturgy, has always been part of our tradition.

"Auricular," when it is not used medically to talk about our ears, means "understood or recognized by the sense of hearing," with the derivative meaning, "told privately." In other words, the confessor, like the spiritual director, is a holy listener. Her task is to pay attention, to hear what is said and what is left unsaid. The sacrament is not private since all sacraments, even when only two persons are present, are celebrated within the church; here the priest represents the whole community of the faithful. In the sacrament of reconciliation, however, the *circumstances* of the telling and hearing are private, and confidentiality is inviolable.

Tucked away in the middle of the 1979 *Book of Common Prayer* are two forms of the rite for the Reconciliation of a Penitent. The first is brief and similar to the Roman Catholic rite (BCP 447-448). The priest listens as witness and judge. This sounds stark and severe, but there is provision for her to "offer counsel, direction, and comfort" after the penitent has named his sins. In my experience this form is not so much harsh as clear and straightforward. For those who make their confession regularly, it is an old friend.

The second form shows the influence of Orthodox Christianity, particularly in the use of the *Trisagion*—"Holy God, Holy and Mighty, Holy Immortal One, have mercy upon us"—said by both priest and penitent at the beginning of the rite (BCP 449-452). There is an atmosphere of mutuality and concelebration; the priest is present as a witness, representing the whole church, but also as a fellow sinner. After passages from scripture have been read, the penitent is reminded that the confession is to be made "in the presence of Christ" and almost secondarily in the presence of "his minister." The tone is pastoral rather than juridical, with the confession itself framed by the story of the prodigal son. Since this parable ends with the father's welcoming his lost child with a feast and an embrace, the emphasis throughout is implicitly on God's love rather than on the penitent's sinfulness. The rite provides for the laying on of hands when the absolution is spoken, suggesting both healing and blessing.

In either rite the priest may assign a penance—another word with an uncomfortable aura for most of us, suggesting some ascetical feat such as kneeling on gravel while reciting the Lord's Prayer or sleeping on nails for the forty days of Lent. Or it may suggest an almost mechanical exercise, prescribed for all regardless of the gravity of their sins: Say six Hail Marys and three Our Fathers—the sacramental equivalent of "Take two aspirin and call me in the morning." To be sure, the root of the word "penance" is the Latin *poena*, which can be variously translated as punishment, retribution, or recompense. Medieval penitential guides make it clear that, in the good old days, penance could be painful and costly: severe fasts, floggings, dangerous pilgrimages, and imprisonment.

Yet the purpose of penance is not so much punishment as satisfaction, righting insofar as possible the wrong that has been done, and amendment, some action indicative of the intent to lead a new life. A good penance is short, performable, and does not attract attention. It may involve restitution, when this is possible without relieving the conscience of the penitent while creating new burdens for the person sinned against. Sometimes old wounds are better left unopened. I prefer a penance that is really an act of thanksgiving, such as meditating on a verse of scripture that assures us of God's love. Psalm 18:20 is one of my favorites: "He brought me out into an open place; he rescued me because he delighted in me."

God's love and delight in us is, after all, what confession is all about. It is easy to overlook this truth and to become preoccupied with our own sinfulness. Yet the sacrament of reconciliation is so named because, when the penitent's sins are put away, she is restored and reconciled to "the blessed company of [God's] faithful people" (BCP 450). Absolution is not forgiveness: only God—and the people we have wronged—can forgive our sins. Rather, it is an assurance and certification that our sins *are* forgiven. The penitent is then obliged to let them go—which is not always easy!

There are really two kinds of confession. There is the occasional use of the sacrament, when the penitent is burdened, often by a very specific sin that is usually a sin of action rather than a sinful way of being. This is the stuff of movies and television dramas—should the priest turn in the confessed murderer or thwart the terrorist bomber, even if this means breaking the unbreakable seal? In real life, the situation is rarely so dramatic, but making one's confession can bring closure and relief from the very real pain of unacknowledged sin.

The other kind is "devotional confession," that is, confession made regularly as part of one's spiritual discipline. Typically, Advent and Lent are the seasons for such use of the sacrament, although some may prefer greater frequency. For those who hear confessions themselves, it is imperative that they make their own confession at least once a year. For the rest of us, devotional confession may or may not be a meaningful spiritual exercise, something to consider prayerfully and to discuss with a trusted friend or director.

The first time is the hardest, since this initial confession takes in the penitent's whole life. It is a good idea to make an appointment, letting the priest know that this will be a life confession so that sufficient time can be allowed. Then comes the work of reflection and preparation: What will I say? Do I have to remember *everything?* Obviously, some editing is required; I wince at the image of the penitent's saying, after three hours of intense narration, "And then when I was twelve, I...." Instead you might well look at your life by decades or stages, possibly noting significant "stepping-stones" along the way.

Almost always, the same sins turn up in different guises, perhaps more wily and sophisticated with the passing years. My earliest memory of my own marked lack of charity was my vehement refusal to relinquish an apple, supposedly my gift to the Sunday school Thanksgiving basket for the local orphans' home. I did not even want the apple; I just did not want to give it up. Over the decades I have become more subtle, nicer perhaps, but still working on true generosity. This tendency toward repetition is not the same as willfully committing the same sin over and over. Rather, most of us have a "besetting sin," which is like an area of weakness or predisposition, just as some of us catch colds easily while others tend to break out in rashes. It is a sad truth that sin, serious as it is, is basically boring.

There are all sorts of little books, some good and some not, to help in preparation. I often suggest that the penitent look for areas of disproportion: "What is out of order? Where am I out of sync?" Or she might reflect: "Where do I hurt?" This may seem simplistic, but we frequently hurt because we have let ourselves become separated from God. And, of course, it is almost always useful to look at our motivations and behaviors in the light of the Ten Commandments. It helps to make a few notes, though not a great compendium, being sure to destroy the list after the confession has been made.

Some parishes post regular times for confessions, but more commonly it is necessary to make an appointment. I am most comfortable hearing confessions in my study, where I can be sure that there will be no interruptions or observers, but some priests prefer the church nave or a side chapel. While traditionally the priest sits and the penitent kneels, a comfortable conversational setting is increasingly common; the situation is sufficiently awe-inspiring of itself without the heightened drama of special postures. The confessor normally listens without interrupting and asks questions only for clarification, never out of curiosity. He helps the penitent distinguish true sins from peccadillos and mishaps; most of us have an amazing tendency to get them tangled together. He is a safe and welcoming presence.

Theoretically, the person of the confessor does not matter. In practical terms, however, it matters a great deal. The confessor should be someone whose discretion is trusted, who regularly makes her own confession, and who is able to reflect the love of Christ while taking sin with the utmost seriousness. Because the rite is a sacrament, confessions are normally heard by priests. To be sure, lay chaplains and spiritual directors hear many confessions that are not officially labeled as such since they cannot offer absolution, though they can assure the penitent of God's forgiveness. Unfortunately, not all priests are comfortable or skilled in exercising this ministry. Like spiritual directors, gifted confessors are born, not made. We would scarcely entrust our bodies to a physician chosen from the Yellow Pages; the cure of souls is an equally important and delicate business. Finding a confessor—like finding a spiritual director—calls for observation, intuition, and some careful inquiries.

PART 2

Praying in the Midst of Life

Chapter Six

Finding God in the Ordinary

Your Kitchen Will Teach You Everything

I have never met anyone who is enthusiastic about housework. Even Brother Lawrence, a monk who lived in the seventeenth century and is frequently invoked as patron of humble household labor because of his classic book *The Practice of the Presence of God,* did not claim to like it although he tolerated fifteen years in a Carmelite kitchen. Domestic science is the grand name once given to glorify or mask the drudgery, and to be sure, some aspects of housekeeping give pleasure. On those days when my life slows down a little, it is a joy to walk to the Korean market on Broadway, surveying the vegetables and fruits and picking only the worthiest, and then to spend a leisurely hour listening to music as I chop and peel and stir. The preparation of a good meal can be a sensory delight and a contemplative respite. In my younger days, when ironing still loomed weekly as an inescapable chore, there was a certain satisfaction in watching the pile of sodden bundles grow steadily smaller while the array of immaculately smooth garments and linens grew steadily larger. But it was a mild satisfaction at best, disproportionate to the hours of hot, mindless labor that had produced it.

The spirituality of housework is largely unexplored, indeed rarely acknowledged. What could God have to do with dirty dishes and dusty furniture? For that matter, what could God have to do with overgrown lawns and clogged gutters, with cluttered basements and messy garages? What could anything so ordinary possibly have to do with the practice of prayer?

Housework—like much of the work that fills our days—is repetitive, cyclical, and could almost always be done better. However important or necessary it might be for the tasks and activities of daily life to run smoothly, housework requires little mental energy, although substantial management skills are necessary if the work is to be done effectively and with economy of effort. In my years as an administrator, I drew steadily on my decades of housewifery, a secret never shared with the institution that employed me. Offices and kitchens have a lot in common.

Our society places little value on housework, and housework well done is generally taken for granted. It is expected to be invisible, to appear effortless. I recall a magazine article that I read shortly after my marriage in the mid-1950s: the good wife was advised to do the vacuuming when her husband was out of the house so that he would not be disturbed by the noise! Supermarket magazines are somewhat more emancipated now, but the tacit message is still there: all that monotonous work is somehow just supposed to *happen*—a whisk here and a whisk there, and comfort, sufficiency, and order will be created.

This work is worth nothing in a society that places a dollar value on nearly everything else. Domestic workers, a vanishing breed, are at the bottom of the economic ladder, along with those who care for the very old, the very young, and the very sick. To maintain a clean and orderly environment for others is a poorly paid job, with no prestige whatsoever. Ours is not the world of public television's *Masterpiece Theater* or of Merchant-Ivory films, where domestic work, however menial, had its own dignity. At the very least, the gentry above the stairs recognized their dependence on the drudgery of those below. Nowadays no one has the ambition "to go into service." The very words are an anachronism, offensive to our democratic ears.

In today's world, in which most people work for pay outside the home, domestic chores must be fit into whatever time slots are available. For at least fifteen years I have routinely done the laundry in the evening after dinner, with my inner clock telling me to stop reading or writing and to trot off at precisely the crucial moment to deal with the washer or dryer. It could not count as "real" work, I thought, since I had the machines to help me and I was not being paid to do it. One day I realized that my working day often extended until bedtime—and even though I "knew better," I still felt compelled to minimize (even to myself) the importance of the homely tasks, tucked in the cracks and tacked on to the end of the "real" working day.

I have been using housework as a metaphor for most of the work that fills our days—routine, usually necessary, and practically never enthralling. Housework is what I know best, the work at which I chafe, sometimes silently and sometimes noisily. It has been the invisible work of women throughout the ages. Yet I could as easily have chosen the factory assembly line, the supermarket checkout register, or the Department of Motor Vehicles as my metaphoric workplace. Even the demanding work of astronauts and neurosurgeons must at some point become humdrum, with hours and days of routine punctuated by moments of exhilarating challenge. For all of us—artists and bus drivers alike—much of the time our work seems not to matter in God's great plan. Does God care about the ordinary tasks of our days? What is the spiritual worth of humble tasks, endlessly repeated?

～ The Cell

Abba Moses of Scete, who surely did his own housework in the fourth-century Egyptian desert, said, "Go to your cell, and your cell will teach you everything." While his life in the desert was extraordinary in its austerity, it was very ordinary in its tedium. Each day must have been like every other day, with prayer at its center and occasional grudging conversation with those spiritual seekers who kept turning up despite the inhospitable environment. There was an unrelenting cycle of physical labor as well, to procure just enough food and water for survival. As they prayed, the abbas supported themselves by plaiting ropes and mats for sale or exchange—surely a labor as repetitive as ironing or scrubbing. Like all good housewives, they were able to do two things at once. It was a life stripped down to the barest minimum.

Abba Moses and his brothers realized both the challenge and the potential holiness of this radically simplified environment and lifestyle. Go to your cell, he commanded, not because it is comfortable or interesting, but because there you must face your own solitude, indeed your own self. Abba Moses knew the dangers of tedium, of deadly sameness. He knew the perils of the sin of *acedia*, known to the desert dwellers as the noonday devil. The bare little cell was the place for the encounter with God, but it was also the place for the encounter with boredom, dullness, and the sin of sloth. *Acedia* sounds more elegant, but it is plain old sloth, the sluggish sin that pulls us down and deadens our souls.

The cell became the arena for the struggle, as the desert fathers fought the temptation to yield to the noonday devil, which was to abandon their passionate longing for God. I suspect that most of them were more than a little crazy. They were certainly bizarre and difficult people, yet there is a stark honesty in many of their sayings. If we refuse to be put off by their harshness and eccentricity, they are surprisingly contemporary in their insights. They knew that God was to be encountered in the ordinary, requiring no special trappings of comfort and beauty. They knew that God was to be found right there, in the bleakness of the little cell.

When I am overwhelmed with everydayness and burdened with the tedious tasks of ordinary living, I find it hard to pray. Then I tell myself, "If only you didn't have so much to do, if only you had more time, if only you could get out of this predictable, boring routine and go to some really *spiritual* place, like a monastery or a desert—then it would be easy to pray." Even as I think this, though, I know that my monastic friends would be quick to disabuse me of this idea, were I so naive as to share it with them.

In my heart I know that Abba Moses was right: go to your cell, and your cell will teach you everything. Go to your kitchen, and your kitchen will teach you everything. Go to your office, and your office will teach you everything. Go to your classroom, and your classroom will teach you everything. Go to the place of your daily work—whether it be an office in the executive suite or the checkout line at the supermarket—and you will find all the spiritual challenge and promise you can manage. The noonday devil is there, waiting for a good hand-to-hand tussle. God can be met there too, but sometimes it is harder to perceive his presence because his opponent is a genius at diverting our attention.

The noonday devil is gray and shabby, nothing like Milton's splendid Lucifer. He is thoroughly at home in the ordinary and quite expert in the unspectacular, tacky sins of the everyday. Most of our sinning, after all, is threadbare and unimaginative, as repetitive as the desert abbas' spinning their ropes and weaving their mats. The noonday devil can tempt us to little acts of meanness and impatience. He can encourage our ugly little spurts of envy and persuade us that only the uptight pay much attention to the sins of gluttony and lust. Perhaps most insidious of all, the noonday devil can insinuate himself into our thoughts, suggesting that God is not very interested in us and that consequently what we do is not important. He can persuade us that all that matters is the confining here and now, so we might as well let go of dreams and hopes. If we tolerate his presence in our cell, we become leaden and spiritually dead.

Back in the 1960s I taught Goethe's *Faust* to college students who were probably more interested in mind-altering chemicals than in early nineteenth-century drama. To me, Mephistopheles, like Milton's Lucifer, is the most interesting character in the play. He is endlessly resourceful, with a mordant sense of humor that would make him a welcome addition to any flagging party. *Faust* turned up in my syllabus every April, and for a long time I had difficulty taking Mephisto seriously as the embodiment of evil—he was just too *ordinary*. Then I became aware of one crucial little sentence, in which he identifies himself to Faust: "I am the spirit of eternal negation."

In other words, "I don't need magic tricks or scary outfits. I can just stay beside you and keep saying 'No.' I can try to quench the God-spark within you or I can keep wheedling until you try to quench it yourself. You'll end up doing all the work while I just watch and keep you company." That sounds to me suspiciously like the noonday devil.

Whatever the physical dimensions of our desert cell or suburban kitchen or high-tech office, their spiritual space is simultaneously constrictive and expansive beyond all imagination. The workplace can stultify or it can be a holy place where we stretch and grow and glimpse the infinite. Life in the cell can pique our divine restlessness and at the same time satisfy it.

The restlessness is important. The cell is not a hiding place and need not be a prison, however trapped we sometimes feel in the inexorable routine of daily work. Rather, it can be an arena, for to seek God there is to struggle. To seek God there is to turn our backs on the noonday devil as we say "No" to the spirit of negation. To seek God in the cell is to be alone with ourselves, even when we are surrounded by family and fellow workers. To seek God in the cell demands that we be unflinching in our willingness to know ourselves. This is more than a self-indulgent "getting in touch with our feelings." It is to look deeply into ourselves and to become aware of our capacity for both good and evil. It is to accept our nothingness and yet to be able to value ourselves as made in God's image.

The inextricable link between knowledge of ourselves and knowledge of God is well established in Christian tradition, articulated with special clarity by the spiritual writers of fourteenth-century England. Thus Julian of Norwich, who was an astute psychologist as well as a mystic and anchorite, writes in her *Showings:*

> For our soul is so deeply grounded in God and so endlessly treasured that we cannot come to knowledge of it, until we first have knowledge of God, who is the Creator to whom it is united....And all of this notwith-

standing, we can never come to the full knowledge of God until we first clearly know our own soul.[1]

Her contemporary, the plain-spoken author of *The Cloud of Unknowing*, knew that coming to knowledge of the soul was hard work:

> So labour and toil as much as you can and know how, to acquire for yourself the true knowledge and experience of yourself as the wretch that you are. And then I think that soon after you will have a true knowledge and experience of God as he is: not as he is in himself, for no one can experience that except God himself...but in as much as this is possible, and as it is his good pleasure to be known and experienced by a humble soul living in this mortal body.[2]

For both Julian and the author of the *Cloud*, the fruit of time in the cell is self-knowledge, which is the only way truly to come to the knowledge of God. Thus the time we spend doing menial or repetitive tasks and the work we undertake day after day, far from being wasted time, is part of our life of prayer. This life in the cell—and in the kitchen and the tollbooth on the Interstate—calls for patience and persistence. Woody Allen's maxim, "Ninety percent of life consists in showing up," expresses a deep truth about the heroism of the ordinary. Faithfulness rarely feels heroic; it feels much more like showing up and hanging in. It is a matter of going to our cell, whatever form that might take, and letting it teach us what it will.

In our imagination, we can imbue the cell of the fourth-century desert with a certain romantic aura. Dis-

1. *Showings*, 288-289.
2. *Cloud*, 150.

tance in time and place creates a pleasant haziness, and the tormenting challenges of heat and thirst recede. Our twentieth-century cell, however, does not invite romanticism, and its challenges are quite apparent to us. Present-day offices, those little cubicles with flimsy partial walls and minimal, functional furniture, look very much like cells. They provide no place for either beauty or eccentricity and certainly no place for the solitude of the desert. There is plenty of cool, potable water just down the hall, and the temperature is controlled by sophisticated air-conditioning systems. Yet in them we experience isolation rather than solitude, even when the office is a crowded maze of cubicles. Our desert cells can be any of the bleak—or at least neutral—places where tasks are accomplished, goals are met, and paychecks earned. The kitchen can be just a kitchen, the toll booth just a toll booth. Or they can be the place where God is encountered.

Brother Lawrence, our patron of housekeeping, was a hero of the ordinary. For a long time I was tempted to think of him as a kindly old codger pottering around his kitchen and offering bits of pious wisdom—we *do* tend to domesticate our holy people in order to make them easier to live with—but he was actually a wise and strong man. He had been a soldier in the Thirty Years' War, that cruel and confused conflict filled with random atrocities inflicted on soldier and civilian alike. He knew firsthand the horror of violence and the human capacity for evil. He knew about pain from his own body: chronic gout led to an ulcerated leg that for years caused him pain whenever he moved about. And he knew more than he wanted to about day-in, day-out humble work, first in the monastery kitchen and then in the cobbler's shop. He was not always sure how to get the job done, but he relied on God, as his abbot related from a conversation with him:

The same thing was true of his work in the kitchen, for which he had a naturally strong aversion; having accustomed himself to doing everything there for the love of God, and asking His grace to do his work, he found he had become quite proficient in the fifteen years he had worked in the kitchen.[3]

There, in the workplace, Brother Lawrence was profoundly aware of God's presence. He did not so much *say* his prayers as *live* them. In conformity with the rule of his community, he observed the prescribed times for prayer—"he retired to pray when Father Prior told him to do so"—but his holy place was the workplace, not the monastery chapel. His abbot reports his saying that "he was more united to God in his ordinary activities than when he devoted himself to religious activities which left him with a profound spiritual dryness."[4]

While Brother Lawrence knew himself closest to God when he engaged in his ordinary tasks, it is important to remember that he did not *choose* these tasks and that the kitchen work, at least, was especially repellent. He did not *like* what he was doing. Yet this was the work assigned to him, and he was obliged to perform it under his monastic vow of obedience.

Now that is a word to raise our hackles! Most of us do not live under monastic vows, and our mistaken understanding of obedience makes us mistrustful of the very word. The idea of *anyone* compelling us to do *anything* is abhorrent, even as much of the time we find ourselves doing many things that we would rather not do if we had the

---

3. Brother Lawrence of the Resurrection, *The Practice of the Presence of God*, ed. John J. Delaney (New York: Image, 1977), 41.

4. *Ibid.*, 47.

choice. We may not acknowledge it, but often we are acting implicitly under obedience, which is not the exclusive province of monastics. Marriage demands obedience, parenthood demands obedience, jobs demand obedience, and a lively relationship with God demands the most obedience of all.

True obedience has nothing to do with a reflexive response to commands. Neither servile nor self-deprecating, it certainly has nothing to do with the kind of obedience that will teach your dog to attack only on command or at least to walk calmly on a leash. True obedience goes deeper. It cannot be compelled, but rather must be entered into freely. (No one asks the dog whether he wants to learn manners.) Obedience makes us partners in a covenanted relationship, with one another and with God. It is not so much a matter of coercion as attentiveness; traced back to its Latin roots, the verb "to obey" is related to *audire*, "to hear."

To be obedient is to be present and attentive to another, to hear what the other is saying, with words and sometimes without words, and then to respond lovingly and generously. We owe this kind of obedience to all those whom we love and who love us. It is the ground for any fruitful relationship. Hurtful things cannot thrive, but all kinds of good things can flourish when we are carefully attentive to one another.

∾ The Cell of Family Life
Abba Moses' cell lacked creature comforts, but it offered one luxury: he was responsible for himself alone. He was spared the major and minor irritants of family living, which perhaps is one reason he and his fellows took to the desert. I wonder how often they withdrew to their cells, ostensibly to pray but really just to enjoy the solitude—no

questions, no comments, no criticisms, no complaints, no one needing anything *right now*, no one tracking sand across the freshly swept floor. I confess that I find it easy to be good during those days and weeks when I am playing at being a desert mother in Jenkins Hollow. There is no one to annoy me or make demands on me. I cannot complain about traffic noises because there is no traffic on the dirt road. I cannot complain about rude and incompetent service because the nearest country store is five miles away: too far for a casual walk and besides, Wilma does not sell anything I really want. I cannot complain about slow subways because the nearest public transportation is in Charlottesville. The only person I can get cross at is myself, which I do occasionally since too much serenity is hard to take. Most of the time, though, I sit in my cell and purr and love everyone. Of course, there is no one around to get in my way.

In contrast, those who live in families must often sacrifice the pleasure of going all by themselves into their cell so that their cell can teach them everything. Instead, they find themselves making concessions and compromises that would unnerve Brother Lawrence in his single-minded devotion. I wonder how he would have managed getting three children—the lagging, the absent-minded, and the recalcitrant—off to school on time. Would he have remained patient while searching for matching socks and reminding the poky one that she had better be ready to go out the door in five minutes? I recall myself getting progressively crabbier on such mornings and thinking, "Is this supposed to be a spiritual experience? Whoever told me that motherhood was a holy calling?"

The chaotic cell of family life has plenty to teach us, but it is often difficult to clear away the clutter and slow down long enough to pay attention. Instead, all our little sinful ways get activated in the stress of proximity. Our children, even more than our spouses and partners, know the absolute worst about us. We rely on their forgiveness, and they grant it more readily than we deserve.

Further, there is the burden of expectation: the Christian family is supposed to resemble a collage of Norman Rockwell paintings, with maybe a bit of Disney or *Leave It to Beaver* thrown in. In my own June Cleaver days, I would sometimes wonder: can I create that kind of household single-handedly, especially since the others do not seem to have the script? And do I want to? And where is God in this scene anyhow?

Scripture does not offer a great deal of help. When I hear my fundamentalist friends exhorting us to turn back to the Bible to shore up our family values, I think, "What about all those multiple wives and concubines in the Old Testament? And what about Abraham and Sarah? Is that the family we are supposed to emulate?" In my imagination, I like to supply Sarah's part of the dialogue: "Why did you tell that man that I was your sister, not your wife? What do you mean we're moving but you don't have any idea where we're going? What on earth were you doing with Isaac up on the mountain? He's had nightmares ever since you got back." The gospels do not offer much specific help either: Jesus had no compunction about snatching men away from their families and livelihood. No, the Bible is many things, but it is not a handbook on family values.

Yet most of us live in families of one sort or another and strive to achieve the delicate balance of fidelity to our baptismal vows and fidelity to those with whom we are covenanted. Obedience does not come easily! Sometimes we are tempted to walk out on a house full of small children who depend on us or a spouse who no longer enchants us after fifteen years of marriage or an aged and sick parent who needs our care. The idea of a clean sweep and a fresh start can be very attractive, especially if we can blame God for our apparent dereliction. There are times when the cell is teaching us more than we want to know, and we want out! It is not easy to sustain our passion for following God's call in the face of the down-to-earth realities of ordinary family life. Nor is it easy to live into the question: where is God in the nitty-gritty?

Gandhi—who did not have a good track record as a family man—is reported to have said, "If you don't find God in the very next person you meet, it is a waste of time looking for him further." I would add, "If you don't find God in the person who forgets to put the toilet seat down or brings home a disastrous report card or violates the 11:00 P.M. curfew, it is a waste of time looking for God further." Families are social entities, but more importantly they are spiritual communities.

～ Vocation

It can also be difficult to think of the workplace as a spiritual community. To look for God in the irritating fellow worker, the incompetent administrative assistant, or the unwelcoming receptionist is indeed a challenge! To look for God in the drabness of much of our daily work can be even more difficult.

Too often, the demands of everyday living keep us from awareness of God's presence in our lives, as tight schedules and petty irritations threaten to crowd him out. I suspect that we collude in this out of self-consciousness and our Anglican idea of good taste—we fear we will look a little too pious or spiritually pretentious unless we treat God with a distanced politeness. Surely we are not expected to bring him into all the details of daily life? It is easier to call on God in church during visiting hours than to acknowledge the divine presence in the kitchen or the garage.

Yet scripture tells us that our tenacious God sticks with us and intrudes himself into the moments of our daily lives. After all, he keeps track of falling sparrows and knows us right down to the number of hairs on our head. God is the one to whom all hearts are open, all desires known—even the unworthy ones—and from whom no secrets are hid—even the embarrassing, shameful and silly ones. Our task, if we choose to accept it—to borrow a familiar line from *Mission Impossible*—is to grow in awareness of the God-component in our everyday life. This is not an impossible mission, but it most certainly is a risky one: we might be forced to grow, to change, and to forgive. We might have to learn more about loving each other, loving God, and loving ourselves. We might have to learn the most difficult lesson about loving: how to accept the love of God, especially as it comes to us mediated through the fallible people who share our life. Like the heroes of the old television show, we are free not to accept the mission, and we have many ways of saying "no" to that love.

Obedience kept Brother Lawrence faithfully in his kitchen and cobbler's shop. Obedience to our daily tasks, especially obedience promised in the sight of God and the Christian community, can keep us faithful in our equivalent of the kitchen. It can sanctify the ordinary and transform the burdens of obligation into the joy of vocation: I am not simply stuck here, I am *called*.

In my sophomore year in high school, "Vocations" was a required course. (If it still exists, it is probably called Career Choices.) In our little school in a backwater corner of Kansas City, we spent a semester pondering our futures: what job is right for me? The teacher's role was to direct us toward the right slots. The academically slow must not as-

pire too high—Shirley Barry, the best volleyball player in
the school, thought she might become a brain surgeon and
had to be rerouted. The capable must be prodded to aspire a
little higher—my I.Q. moved me out of the nurse category
into the doctor class, but that created problems because I
was a girl. I doubt that anyone, Mrs. Hoy included,
thought much about how the course got its name and how
exciting it might be if we really wrestled with the challenge
and wonder of being *called*. We unremarkable adolescents
might have glimpsed the almost infinite expansiveness of
our cells whatever they might turn out to be. We might
even have glimpsed the possibility of heroism.

You do not have to look like Brother Lawrence to be a
hero of the ordinary. They come in all sizes, shapes, and
colors. I met one recently disguised as a man named Michael, who is a computer repairman down in Culpeper, the
nearest town to Jenkins Hollow. Working with his hands,
keen eyes, and almost intuitive knowledge of their intricacies, he does more than fix ailing machines. He brings to his
work an unassuming quality of ministry and care. Even as
he shakes off my effusive thanks for having saved my life,
he knows that what he does in his cluttered workroom
matters. "I knew you were writing something, and I knew
you were worried about losing it, so I wanted to get it fixed
as quick as I could. I'm glad we"—generous man to share
the credit, surely not with me, but maybe with God—"figured out what was wrong."

Like Michael, who goes under the pseudonym Data-
man, the heroes of the ordinary are all sorts and conditions
of men and women who are able to see, if only intermit-
tently, that they are known and loved by God and that as a
consequence their daily work can be their calling and their
prayer. They know that God is with them in unlikely and
seemingly barren places.

Behind the old house in Jenkins Hollow are the remains of a mill. The top story is gone, and the millstone and the water wheel disappeared long ago, but the impressive stone structure remains. There is no roof, trees are growing up inside it, and we have found hundreds of bottles tossed there by the master-moonshiner who lived here before us. The workmanship is beautiful: the heavy stones are fit together, intricately and without mortar. The building will be there long after I am dead. I found the date 1810 carved on one of the stones; it is so faint that it will be gone before too long. We have been told that the mill was built by slaves hired out from the big plantation down the road. I think of them, especially on hot days when the insects are biting and I know that copperheads and rattlers are lurking in the tall grass. Did they have shoes? How did they move those heavy stones? And how did they know how to fit them together so tightly that they would have a solid building and not a rock pile?

At least one of those nameless men was kin to Brother Lawrence, for carved on a stone near the entrance are the words, "I love Jesus." Afflicted and burdened though he was, he somehow managed to make his work his prayer. In conditions of great hardship, he managed to find a calling where others might have found only slavery.

It is good to live in consciousness of blessing, God's little surprises that are embedded in the most ordinary days. A Jewish colleague told me about the prayer to be said in thanksgiving for new things, first things. He is not observant, but he makes it a point to go outdoors with his children and say the prayer at the first snowfall each year. It is more about acknowledging blessing than giving thanks, although gratitude is implicit in our awareness. I remember when I first felt my child move within me; it was faint, scarcely perceptible, but it was a moment of blessing.

I remember sitting at the round oak table eating strawberry shortcake, made with berries I had picked and my mother's rich biscuit (which she declared anybody could make, and I have never been able to duplicate)—lots of calories, but lots of blessing too. In Jenkins Hollow it is a holy moment when the Great Blue Heron pauses to fish from our low water bridge. The list could go on and on—the unconditional love of small children, the gracefulness and innocence of animals, all the bits of blessing waiting to be noticed. I think I see more as I get older, possibly because each day is more precious. We might find it too intense to be aware of God and God's wonders every minute of the day, although Brother Lawrence seems to have managed.

~ Chapter Seven

Parenting and Prayer

How Do I Pray When the
Baby is Keeping Me Up?

One of the most common and yet profound ways both men and women grow in their spiritual lives is through parenthood. Through parenting they become aware that the creation of life in conception and birth is a participation in the creativity of the Creator God; the care of a helpless newborn becomes a way of understanding the love of a nurturing God. Pregnancy and childbirth can be times filled with wonder and awe, particularly for women: the first faint brush of inner movement leads her to marvel, "Was that really my child?" Pushing a child out of her own body, about the most undignified and simultaneously most glorious possible feat, and feeding a child from that same body, are experiences that profoundly change our sense of who we are as embodied people.

And true maternity is not necessarily a matter of anatomy or obstetrical experience, as we know from scripture. In the book of Isaiah, God likens himself to a nursing mother; in Luke's gospel, Jesus tells the stubbornly wrongheaded children of Jerusalem that he longs to shelter them as a hen gathers her chicks under her wings. Closer to home, one of the truly maternal figures of my own childhood was my Scottish grandfather. Others may have found him dour, but I knew him as the tender person who held me when I was hurt or frightened, who knew how to make soup and oatmeal, and who was never too tired to read one more story. He was more motherly than most mothers, even my own, whose poor health often made her remote.

In our present time, it is a joy to see fathers carrying their babies close to their bodies in the little cloth carriers aptly called Snugglis, to see them deal deftly and fairly willingly with diapers, and to witness unabashed displays of affection that would have been deemed "unmanly" by earlier generations. After millennia of exclusion from the mysteries of birth and child care, fathers are being invited to share at least some of the experiences that were traditionally the province of mothers. They may not be able to give birth, but they can share from the very beginning the demanding—and sacred—work of caring for their babies and small children. They too suffer broken sleep and participate in the seemingly endless cycle of daily care. They are learning about mothering. My grandfather was way ahead of his time!

And yet parenting, like any experience that changes our lives so profoundly, brings with it tension and upheaval. It can be so difficult to find our equilibrium again, and we lose a sense of relationship to God when our days are filled with what can seem to be distractions in caring for little ones. Our ways of praying—if we manage to pray at all—change; our whole understanding of God is brought into question. Such was the case for my friend Jenny.

〜 Childbirth and Prayer

Jenny had always impressed me as a natural contemplative. Under the guidance of her parish priest and spiritual director, Tom, she was accustomed to spending several hours in prayer daily. It was as if, like the Samaritan woman, she had been thirsting for years and suddenly, as she approached thirty, discovered the inexhaustible well of God's presence. I loved being around her: her joy and vitality were contagious. But Jenny was not a monastic. She was a bright, highly educated woman who had put aside her own professional aspirations to live the double life of affluent suburban wife and closet mystic. She managed gracefully to look and act the part of the former, even as she embarked on a quiet voyage of exploration to her spiritual depths.

This was a full and satisfying life and might have been enough, but even as she yearned for God, Jenny also yearned for a child. For several years she and her husband had subjected themselves to all manner of medical tests and regimens, some painful and costly, hoping each month that *this* would be the time and that their much-wanted baby was now at least a promising mass of rapidly dividing cells.

Finally it happened: Jenny called to tell me that she was indeed pregnant, that she felt awful, but that even morning sickness was welcome as an unmistakable sign of her long-delayed fruitfulness. The nine months of waiting became more and more a time of intense, wordless prayer as Jenny simplified her life and turned more deeply inward. Sophie's birth was harder and more painful than the hospital classes had led Jenny to expect, but she was filled with delight at the sight of her tiny girl-child.

I did not hear from Jenny for several weeks after her announcement of Sophie's birth. Then one Monday morning she called and asked if I had a few minutes. When I asked how she was, she burst into tears. "It's terrible. It's like nothing I've ever experienced. I love Sophie, I'd die for her, she's wonderful, but she *never* sleeps. I feel so awful that I'm not happier, that it's so hard to take care of her, but I'm exhausted. I shouldn't be crying. I should be happy. I *am* happy, but it's all so hard. And Margaret, I'm not praying. I haven't prayed since she was born. I know I should be praying, but I can't find the time."

I found myself in my pragmatic peasant mode: "Forget about the prayer for a minute, and tell me—are you eating?"

"No," she wailed, "I haven't time for that. I haven't even time to wash my face."

We talked for a few minutes about things that Jenny knew—cognitively, at least, if not in her depths: how newborns are exhausting, how giving birth throws the mother into hormonal chaos, how parenting has to be learned like any other skill. I reminded her that, unbelievable as it might seem at the moment, Sophie would some day sleep through the night and eat three meals a day at predictable times, that indeed someday she would experiment with makeup and fall in love with scruffy teenagers.

"I know," Jenny said, "but I should at least be able to pray. Before Sophie was born, I spent hours every day just centering and being attentive to God. I talked to my priest last week, and he reminded me that prayer is *so* important, it's the basis of *everything* in my life, so I just have to find time for it—somehow. I keep trying, but I just can't. I feel like a fake and a failure. I can't do anything right! I used to feel so close to God. I thought I'd call you; maybe you'll know what I'm talking about and maybe you can tell me what to do. I feel like I've lost God, just when I should feel close to him. I'm not sure Tom knows much about new babies. I just couldn't make him understand how tired I am."

From his response to Jenny's plight I was pretty sure that Tom's experience with neonatals was distant, if it existed at all, but I resisted the temptation to disparage a fellow priest. Instead, Jenny and I talked for a long time about the physical—and spiritual—realities of motherhood. She had had no difficulty comprehending the wonder of Sophie's conception after years of yearning, and she had experienced the birth itself, however difficult, as a glimpse of the numinous. But now the drama was over, and she was left with a demanding, querulous infant. Her days and nights centered around feeding and diapering, diapering and feeding, with snatches of sleep scarcely refreshing because they were cruelly unreliable. God seemingly had been crowded out, or perhaps had never been there. The old ways no longer worked, and the possibility of order emerging from the fatigue and chaos of the present seemed absurd: in the microcosm of Jenny's life, it was an apocalyptic time.

∿ Parenting and Prayer

Talking with Jenny made clear to me once again how much of our spiritual tradition and literature is based on a monastic model and how much spiritual violence we inflict on ourselves when we force ourselves into a procrustean discipline mistaken for prayer. In the Middle Ages, Jenny would have made a splendid abbess. Perhaps in the fourth century, she would have been a wise and holy woman of the desert. In our own time, had her life begun in a different tradition and taken a different course, she might be a member of an enclosed contemplative community. But she was none of these; rather, she was a young woman living in a comfortable house in a pleasant suburb. Jenny's life was full and complex. No ascetic, she enjoyed beautiful things and a rich variety of relationships. Until Sophie's birth, she was blessed with sufficient leisure to live by a quasi-monastic rule of prayer while outwardly conforming to the expectations of her husband and the community.

Jenny had not anticipated the radical change that the birth of a child would bring to her life. She was not prepared for the unpredictability of life with a newborn and the accompanying loss of spontaneity. As we talked, I was flooded with the memory of my arrival home from the hospital with my firstborn. I had placed her gingerly in the crib and then flung myself face down on the bed. Like Sophie, my daughter was a loved and wanted child. But as I lay there I thought, "I'll never dance again. I'll just get old taking care of that baby. My life as a free person is over." I was right, but I was also wrong. It was decades before I again enjoyed more than glimmers of the freedom and spontaneity I grieved on that cold November day in a dingy Cambridge student apartment. While my life as a "free person" was not over, it was profoundly transformed and enriched. Rather quickly, I learned that there was more to life than dancing. Even more than a night of uninterrupted sleep.

I told Jenny of my memory, still so vivid that I could feel the crinkles of the thick cotton bedspread pressing into my cheek. She already knew instinctively that I had been where she was that day, but recalling my experience as a new mother united us across the generations. We talked about the inevitable crushing fatigue, the total unpredictability of everyday life, and how the small creature in the crib could dominate and destroy any vestige of a reasonably ordered life.

We talked about the overwhelming *physicality* of life with a new baby. No one had warned me—and no one had warned Jenny—that the early days of motherhood are soggy. Breasts ooze milk, and babies (as one of my childless

academic friends observed) are so incredibly *cloacal*, needing diaper changes throughout the day and night. For a
woman who has lived in her mind or whose spirituality is
grounded in the abstract realm of much traditional prayer,
so much embodiment comes as a rude shock. To be sure,
pregnancy is a time of physical preparation, when the
woman's body seems to take on a will of its own and refuses to be ignored. But pregnancy is also a time of mystery, inwardness, and introspection. New life is contained
within the body, and almost instinctively with each of my
babies I found myself turning inward during the months of
waiting. Who was this unseen, unknown person with
whom I was living so intimately? The changes in my outward appearance were obvious, but the real changes, the
mysterious processes of unfolding new life, were hidden,
contained, and secret. Life with a newborn is something
else—explosive, expansive, and flooded. Flooded with feelings, flooded with tears, flooded with the physical reality of
the newborn child.

Jenny brought us back to the subject: "But how can I
pray when it's all that I can do just to get through the day? I
miss praying, I want to pray, I *need* to pray. It's as if I've lost
a big piece of my life."

I tried to tell Jenny what I had learned from my own
three children, something I wish I had known nearly forty
years ago when the nurse at the hospital door put a
blanket-wrapped bundle into my hands and said, "She's all
yours now. Enjoy!" None of the books I had read or the parenting classes I attended had told me that there is something sacramental in the repetitious, seemingly unending
care of those small, demanding bodies. A sacrament, after
all, is an "outward and visible sign of inward and spiritual
grace."

We know that newborns are sensory creatures, experiencing the world through touch and voice. For them there is no dichotomy of body and soul. They are learning about being human from the hands that touch them and the voices they hear long before words have any meaning. If the hands and voices are gentle and comforting, they are learning about love; indeed, they are receiving intimations of God's love.

"What would happen," I asked myself and Jenny, "if you saw the never-ending, repetitive tasks of motherhood as an opportunity for prayer? If each time you put your hands on Sophie's little body, perhaps to wash or change her, perhaps just to hold and cuddle her, you remembered that you were communicating something powerful and life-filled? Then you might manage a prayer—not some elegant statement in sixteenth-century English or a transcendental moment of numinous experience, but just a simple 'Thank you' or 'Help!' Or maybe nothing with words, but just a moment of awareness of the wonder of bodies and souls, the wonder of a new person growing from the meeting of two cells, and the profound helplessness and need of all God's creatures, most clearly manifest in this few pounds of human flesh touched by your hands right now."

No doubt it was easier for me to say something like this to Jenny in our Monday morning phone conversation and to write it now because I speak from the comfortable perspective of one who has paid her dues. Unless I am miraculously blessed (or afflicted?) like Sarah, I can be sure that my sleep will never again be broken or my work schedule interrupted by the demands of an infant or small child. I am convinced of the truth of my insight, but I know from my own memories and from conversation with young friends that living into it is neither easy nor automatic. Like more traditional forms of prayer, this awareness of the sacramentality and sacredness of caring for newborns calls for faithfulness, even dogged persistence when God seems absent or absent-minded.

∾ The Nurturing God

The experience of caring for a newborn is a good time to explore our mental pictures of God. To whom am I praying? What picture of the ultimately unknowable God informs my prayer? Is it the God who smites the ungodly and whose anger is easily kindled, the God of whom the psalmist writes, "Smoke rose from his nostrils and a consuming fire out of his mouth; hot burning coals blazed forth from him" (Psalm 18:9)? Such a deity, powerful to be sure, would scarcely be a welcome presence in the family circle right now. More accessible perhaps is the God of Isaiah, who clearly knows what it is like to be a mother and comforts Zion with this promise: "Can a woman forget her nursing child, or show no compassion for the child of her womb? Even these may forget, yet I will not forget you" (Isaiah 49:15).

This is vivid maternal imagery, almost uncomfortable in its evocation of physical intimacy. I remember struggling with it once when I preached a homily on this passage to a largely male congregation. "Should I tell them the truth?" I wondered. "Do they have any idea how impossible it is for a mother to forget a nursing child? I wonder if they're up to hearing the messy details. Do they know that you *hurt*, that you pace the floor, that you can think of nothing else if your breasts are overflowing and the baby isn't there to fulfill his part of the contract?"

Feeding is a powerful symbol of need and generosity. For the infant it is a matter of life and death: survival depends on the willingness of the mother to give of herself. It is also a matter of comfort in its deepest sense, as the child is held securely in the mother's arms, close to her, flesh touching flesh, sheltered by her body. It is no accident that breasts are where they are. This is a time of teaching and learning, as the mother and child look into each other's faces. Hers is the first face the child knows and recognizes. From her face the child learns to smile. From her face the child learns to be human. Looking into her face, the child learns about love and begins to learn about God.

It is important to remember that this is an almost symbiotic relationship, an intimate living together of two different organisms in a mutually beneficial relationship. It is no wonder that child care writers and psychoanalytic theorists speak of "the nursing couple." The mother cannot forget or somehow misplace the infant. To do so would cause her profound discomfort, indeed physical pain. In this mysterious relationship of giving and receiving, she simply cannot opt out and walk away. She is a participant, not merely a provider but also a recipient of comfort.

The love of the mother for her nursing infant is presented in scripture as the most reliable, consistent, and constant way of loving. It is something we all yearn for—to be so known, so tenderly held, and never forgotten. Jenny and indeed all harried and fatigued parents of small infants might do well to address their prayers, their nonprayers, their sighs and complaints to a faithful mothering God who at least understands what they are up against.

They might also let themselves lean against the God imagined by the psalmist when their own capacity for nurturing seems exhausted:

I do not occupy myself with great matters,
  or with things that are too hard for me.
But I still my soul and make it quiet,

> like a child upon its mother's breast,
>> my soul is quieted within me. (Psalm 131:2-3)

This child is no longer a nursing infant, but rather a toddler. Like the toddler, we lead busy lives, running hither and thither, and falling flat from time to time. We can be hopelessly wrongheaded and shortsighted, and we can be overwhelmed by our frustrations and helplessness. Like the toddler, we can be restored by our willingness to rest and let ourselves be held. Jenny yearned to be held, just for a little while; that is why she phoned me. I am sure that all of us—not only the parents of very young children—yearn to be held, spiritually cuddled, and kept safe. So why not direct our prayers to that generous God who invites us to climb into his motherly lap?

⟿ Surviving Parenthood

Jenny was experiencing motherhood at its most intense. As every new parent knows but none can anticipate, the first weeks are unique in their demands and intensity. However, parenthood brings irrevocable changes to the spiritual life that persist far beyond the fatiguing and often chaotic early days when there seems literally no time for prayer, indeed when the new parent lives gingerly from moment to moment and hour to hour.

For one thing, life with infants and very small children is hard on the mind. My first child was born nine months after my successful defense of my doctoral dissertation. I had been accustomed to long periods of uninterrupted reading and writing with unbroken concentration. I had taken for granted the hours of multisyllabic conversations with colleagues. For a few months, once the first hard weeks were past, when like Jenny I had scarcely time to wash my face, it actually seemed possible to have some of the best of both worlds. For part of each day, I would reclaim my old identity while Elizabeth slept or lay propped beside me comfortably in her carrier. When she demanded conversation, she was quite content to hear excerpts of whatever I was reading or to participate in a one-sided discussion of my burning academic issues.

But the human infant is born to communicate, so before very long Elizabeth demanded to become an active partner. It was as if she had understood the condescension in my tossing her verbal scraps. She demanded to be seen, heard, and addressed as an unfolding personality and intellect. An occasional arcane, adult communication was all right, but it was clear that we needed to *talk*. And on her level.

It is probably a good spiritual exercise to talk as peers with preverbal children. They keep us clear and simple. They remind us how funny, sometimes how pathetic we are when we hide behind big words and convoluted grammar. They remind us how delightful sounds can be for their own sake. One of my very young friends, not yet a year old, has been helping me rediscover my lost gifts for vocalizing. He specializes in odd palatal sounds with a slight nasal touch. "Nnnng!" he proclaims. I try it: "Nnnng!" He laughs encouragingly, and the conversation continues with me feeling somewhat like Eliza Doolittle being tutored by Professor Higgins. Occasionally I think, "Good grief, I should be teaching him to talk, and instead he's teaching me his language."

Such interactions are winsome, but leave us depleted and starving if they constitute our total diet. To be sure, it is exciting and intellectually challenging to encourage a child's mind to grow and unfold. But the lack of the stimulus of adult conversation can be spiritually as well as intellectually stunting to new parents. When my own children were small most young mothers did not work outside the home, and activities for women in the church were narrowly circumscribed: service on the altar guild, working on the bazaar, and attendance at ladies' luncheons were the norm. A group of us in our parish reached out spontaneously to one another: "We've got to talk in sentences longer than four words. We've got to talk with people over two feet tall. We've got to be forced to think about something more demanding than diapers and teething. We need books more challenging than *The Cat in the Hat.*"

We swam against the current and encountered the wrath of the parish matrons when we declined to participate in the approved ladies' activities. Our little group had no name, no officers, no by-laws. Twice a month we met in the evening, in someone's living room, after the children were in bed. We read Dietrich Bonhoeffer and C. S. Lewis. We turned our attention to issues of racial and economic injustice, albeit in the politely distanced way of the comfortable middle class. Well ahead of our time, we worried about the environment. We talked! We kept the reputation of young rebels even after we were joined by several women with older children and even a grandmother. After several years, the group—still without a name or formal structure—began gently to dissolve. Some of us went back to school, some returned to paid employment. After nearly thirty years, though, several of us are still loosely in touch but warmly bound together.

That circle of women friends was not a prayer group, yet it was spiritually nourishing. Our minds were hungry, and we ached to stretch them. Our identities as adults were shaky, and we needed to shore them up. I wish, however, that we had been able to ask the God-questions directly, to talk with one another about our loneliness, uncertainties, and seeming abandonment as openly as Jenny can today. I wish we had been able to challenge our images of God and push out the boundaries of our faith. Yet those were other times, and, on balance, we cared for and supported one another. That was probably enough.

We always need our spiritual friends, but we need them especially as parents of infants and small children. This is a time, particularly in the early days and months, when the circle grows very small and days and nights can be very lonely. This is a time when those who have already traveled the road can offer support and companionship. We are gaining wisdom and sensitivity in our dealings with the bereaved; increasingly, there are books and workshops and specialists to guide us. The same need for intentional befriending and care exists at life's other threshold. New parents and all the rest of us, including the childless, would do well to remember that babies and brand new nuclear families do not exist in isolation. Spiritually and emotionally, if not physically, we can share in their nurture. We can encourage parents as they find their way, and we can welcome the newest members into the community.

Life with a very small infant provides a glimpse of what it must be like to be God. To the newborn, the parent—particularly the mother—*is* God. The power of parenthood is awesome. The choice is offered a thousand times a day: to nurture or to neglect, to love or to abuse? There are few other times when we hold such absolute power in our hands. Even the young child has some resources for survival, but the infant is at the mercy of his custodians. Truly, this approaches the power of a deity—and most of us lack the qualifications.

I suspect that some of our horror at accounts of child abuse arises from our awareness of our own potential for sin. Much as we might like to deny it, if we are brave enough to look deep within and face ourselves squarely, it is all too easy to see ourselves in the cruel or neglectful caregiver. If we are honest, we can acknowledge our own times of irritation and impatience along with the occasional, quite surprising dislike of our own offspring. We remember wistfully the time when we were childless and yearn for the freedom and spontaneity that we have lost.

Nevertheless, to be a parent is to be entrusted with frightening power and amazing responsibility. Another lives in complete dependence on us. The potent totality of love is reflected and embodied in the nurture of an infant. To give birth and then to care for the baby—simultaneously powerless in his neediness yet powerful in his will to survive—is to be present at creation. To give birth and then to nurture is to comprehend the wonder of the incarnation. My friend Sally taught me this when she told me about the wonder of her little Sam, a delightful but quite ordinary baby. It was close to Christmas, and we were setting up the creche. "You know, I think just about any baby would have done. They're all holy, at least at the beginning." Maybe she was skirting heresy, but I knew what she meant.

In the years when I did frequent overnight duty as a hospital chaplain, I often found myself drawn to the newborn nursery, where the babies were lined up neatly behind the big window. During the evening visiting hours, parents and grandparents would be there—worshiping. There was no other word for it. The morsels of life in the tiny cribs held the promise of growth and achievement and sin and pain and goodness. Even the funny-looking ones were somehow beautiful. They had done nothing to merit the love that was almost palpably streaming toward them. To love them in their helplessness was thankless work. This was love that made no sense, yet it was love in its truest manifestation. I did not articulate it to myself at the time, but I realize now that I was witnessing something like God's love, love that is unearned and makes no sense. It is not an abstract theological construct, but something very real. It is embodied in the tenderness of ordinary mothers and fathers.

Since we are not God but flawed creatures, we inevitably fall short. The idyllic first few hours of worship through the big nursery window give way to everyday reality, the reality Jenny was experiencing when she called me in desperation. Our best failures lie in the realm of parenting; and our children, who have experienced our love at its most generous and tender, also know us at our worst. They know our impatience and our resentments. They know the anger that we might be able to keep hidden from all others. They know our fallibility and our limitations. Most of the time they manage to love us anyway.

Sophie is in the fourth grade now. She is still a little girl, but a far cry from the helpless infant whose demands left her mother weeping from exhaustion. Jenny has time to pray again. Once again there is time for silence, though not so much as in the childless days. God appears bigger to Jenny now, more mysterious, much more a forgiving mother than a demanding scorekeeper. God and Jenny know each other a lot better than they ever could have without Sophie.

Chapter Eight

Learning Simplicity

'Tis the Gift to Be Simple,
'Tis the Gift to Be Free

I do not like to shop. Malls and department stores over-whelm me, and the perpetual glut of catalogs in my mailbox leaves me giddy. I confess to reading them before I throw them out, feeling just a little guilty, as if they were a kind of spiritual soft porn. At the same time, I also feel a little guilty that I am not doing my share to uphold our consumer economy; by the standards of our secular religion, I do not buy enough. But recently my pride in my commitment to simplicity has been shaken: I bought a new computer and all its accompanying gadgetry.

"Go first class," urged family and friends, "this one will probably see you out." So I studied brightly colored catalogs filled with arcane language about mysterious apparatus and consulted at length with my computer maven, who for a few weeks became a quasi-spiritual director, privy to my hopes, dreams, and fears, and goading me on to embrace new challenges. When the new system was finally in place, it filled one wall of my small study at home and the space beneath the desk was a frightening tangle of cables. According to the manuals—texts written in the same strange language as the catalogs—I was now capable of feats of which I had never dreamed. All I had wanted to do was write letters and journals and modest books, but now I am living with an array of machinery vastly smarter than I and taunting me to move into the twenty-first century. I am still working at befriending my new acquisition, and before long I will even succumb to electronic mail since my friends are losing patience with me.

Part of me is fascinated by the technological wonder that now fills my little room, yet at the same time that wonder makes me sharply aware of how complicated and cluttered my life has become since I went off to college in 1946 with my new Royal portable typewriter. I was on the cutting edge then, the envy of my friends who were still writing term papers by hand. I am not ready to give up my expensive new toy, especially before I have mastered it, but I am nevertheless struck by my apparent duplicity in preaching to myself and others about the spiritual benefits of simplicity.

Simplicity is not one of the cardinal virtues, but perhaps it should be. The old Shaker gift-song tells us that

> When true Simplicity is gained
> To bow and to bend we shan't be ashamed.
> To turn, turn will be our delight,
> 'Till by turning, turning we come 'round right.[1]

This is scarcely a new or radical idea for Christians. Jesus teaches that we should avoid distracting encumbrances: the disciples are sent out without so much as a backpack. They are "to take nothing for their journey except a staff; no bread, no bag, no money in their belts; but to wear san-

---

1. Elder Joseph Brackett, "Inspirational Gift Song," c. 1850, quoted in *The Shakers: Two Centuries of Spiritual Reflection* (New York: Paulist, 1983), 295.

dals and not to put on two tunics" (Mark 6:8-9). This is simplicity carried to the point of austerity and—in my midwestern view—improvidence. I would want at least an umbrella, a change of clothes, and a twenty-dollar bill tucked into a secure pocket. And maybe a few sandwiches. And a credit card. Just in case.

To embrace simplicity calls for a radical trust that does not come easily. Simplicity is not *a* gift; along with the freedom that it brings it is *the* gift. But it must be, in the words of the song, *true* simplicity.

∾ The Work of Simplicity

Simplicity can take on many forms. There is the attractive but studied (and expensive!) simplicity of L. L. Bean and other clothing catalogs. There is also the reactive simplicity of those who reject the complexity of the post-industrial world and yearn to go "back to nature"; we probably all have a bit of Luddite radicalism in us. When my husband and I bought our place in Jenkins Hollow in the mid-1970s, I pored over articles in *Mother Earth News*: would it be ecologically sound and spiritually uplifting to build a privy and get our water from a pump in the yard? I think about those days occasionally as I enjoy a hot shower and wonder how the question ever arose. There is also the simplicity in our eating and drinking, our scheduling of time and our ownership of possessions that is plainly good for us—for our physical and emotional health and for the right use of the world's resources.

The simplicity of the Shaker song and the simplicity both commanded and modeled by Jesus go much deeper. It is not something that we put on or take off. It is not even a way of living that brings physical and emotional health. Rather, it is the core of our identity. It is a way of being that both governs our actions and our attitudes and informs and shapes our prayer.

The gospel writers tell us that Jesus blessed children and used them as a visual aid for his teachings about simplicity. He said to his disciples that unless we change and become like children, we will never enter the kingdom of heaven (Matthew 18:3). Children are complex creatures, to be sure, but they have not yet accumulated the layers that conceal adults and hamper their movements. They can be embarrassingly direct about their desires, unashamed of expressing fear, and unstinting in their affection. Their little boats are relatively free of spiritual barnacles. And yet notice what Jesus tells those of us whose boats are not as unencumbered: "unless you *change....*" In other words simplicity does not just happen; there is conscious work to be done.

To reach this state of childlike openness, it is necessary to strip away whatever blocks our view, hinders our movement, and keeps us from God. Christian tradition uses the term "purgation" to denote that stage of the spiritual life in which we prepare ourselves for greater openness to God by getting rid of all that impedes and distracts us. This process of self-simplification may sound formidable, even punitive, but is in fact liberating. It is as if we take off heavy garments that stifle us and slow us down, or as if we finally cease to stagger under the weight of unnecessary burdens and gently set them aside. As we let go of our clutter—bit by bit, sometimes painfully but often joyfully—we become again as spiritually lithe and agile as children.

Purgation, the exercise of simplicity that frees us of distractions, need not be grim. If we change and become like children, we can recapture the gift of playfulness. Our perspective is restored, for play reminds us of the impermanence of all things: the game may be intense, indeed all-absorbing, but ultimately we know it for what it is—and let go. When we embrace self-simplification with joy, it is hard to make idols of our carefully accumulated toys and trinkets, tangible and intangible, however much we might wish to cling to them.

In order to grow in the spiritual life we have to change—to turn, in the words of the Shaker song—and become as little children. We have to let ourselves accept the extravagant freedom of childhood and recognize the delight of letting go. I remember playing checkers as a child; my older brother outstrategized me and won easily every time. But occasionally we would play "Giveaways" instead of "Keepers," a reversal of the normal order in which the object of the game was to lose as many checkers as rapidly as possibly. The player with no pieces won. The recklessness of the game was exhilarating to me: in order to win it was necessary to throw caution to the winds. I could beat my careful brother every time!

So what are practical ways of cultivating childlike simplicity, some of which will involve little more sacrifice than a weekly visit to the town dump and recycling center? Where are those areas of our lives that merit our attention, that could do with a little tidying up and clearing out?

∼ Simplicity in Possessions

There is great freedom simply in the recognition of our own transience. I realized this not long ago when I bought a new file cabinet for my workroom in the old house in Jenkins Hollow. It is a large, bright room, filled with treasures gathered from the woods and the river and otherwise sparsely furnished with castoff junk. The furniture store in Culpeper was having a sale, and I found a handsome oak cabinet. I could not make up my mind, though: it seemed too good and too solid for my haphazard room. Finally, I said to my husband, "I guess I'll buy it. John [our son] can have it when I'm dead." The saleswoman, hovering nearby, let out a stricken little cry and moved closer—perhaps to catch me when I fell, or to fetch a glass of water or call an ambulance! I assured her that I was in excellent health and was merely looking ahead. I was feeling my impermanence that day and rather enjoyed the resulting sense of lightness.

It is essential that letting go be entered into willingly and with joy. Self-denial is liberating when we are ready for it, but crushing when it is coerced. Voluntary poverty, spiritual or material, bears no resemblance to the brutal deprivation of the ghetto, the prison, or the refugee camp. Rather, it is an intentional relinquishing of anything that separates us from God. As Evelyn Underhill observed,

> The true rule of poverty consists in giving up those things which enchain the spirit, divide its interests, and deflect it on the road to God—whether these things be riches, habits, religious observances, friends, interests, distastes, or desires—not in mere outward destitution for its own sake. It is attitude, not act, that matters; self-denudation would be unnecessary were it not for our inveterate tendency to attribute false value to things the moment they become our own.[2]

On the surface, Evelyn Underhill is an unlikely advocate of poverty. Her outward life was richly complex: as the wife of a successful London marine lawyer, she moved in circles of privilege and affluence. As a scholar, she wrote or edited thirty-nine books, including the definitive *Mysticism,* and over three hundred fifty articles and reviews. In her pictures she is gaunt, almost severe-looking. There are

---

2. *Mysticism,* 211.

no soft lines—I cannot imagine Underhill greeting the poor among whom she ministered (in obedience to her formidable spiritual director Baron Von Hügel) as "My joy."

Yet this middle-aged, middle-class intellectual and dutiful wife led a double, if not a triple life. She was on fire with the love of God. In her writings and in her retreat work—she was a pioneer in introducing retreats to the Church of England—she spoke with compelling warmth and passion. She may have looked like a headmistress, and I am sure that I would have been intimidated by her as a spiritual director. Yet she remains one of the great Anglican voices of our century—and she knew a lot about prayer.

There are, to be sure, humorous bits about her life. Her work of simplification could never have been so radical as she might have wished. She was, after all, Hubert Underhill's wife. She writes to her spiritual director of her attempts to be faithful to her rule of life:

> I am restless and starved when my particular routine is upset. And, during holidays, or when travelling, lecturing, etc.—approximately a quarter of the year—I can't rely on keeping [my rule]. Often no privacy, no certain free time safe from interruption: and the desperate struggle to get it at all costs induces a strain which is hostile to prayer. Lately, in fact, "holidays" have been particular periods of misery on this account. Of course I *never* sacrifice Communions unless they are quite impossible—and even these I cannot be sure of when we are yachting.[3]

Underhill may be the only spiritual giant who owned her own yacht!

---

3. Evelyn Underhill, *Fragments from an Inner Life*, ed. Dana Greene (Harrisburg: Morehouse Publishing, 1993), 136.

In her writings on the spiritual life, Underhill speaks of "self-denudation." This is surely too grand a term for my recent experience of moving from an office that I had occupied for fourteen years, but it was definitely an exercise in simplification. How had so much accumulated in one moderately sized room? Why had I kept it all? Why did I think I needed it? Was I protecting myself by hunkering down in a stronghold of books and papers, or perhaps comforting myself by building a bookish nest? For what? Could I be hiding from God? Lethargy set in as I let the space around me become crowded, promising myself that I would sort it all out—later. The mountains of paper—dreary minutes of long ago meetings, copies of reports and articles filed away unread, and the ubiquitous catalogs—became a symbol of everything about me that was stale, static, and dead. They were an outward and visible sign of inward and spiritual clutter.

I plugged away at preparation for my departure, and then there came a surge of energy, a turning point, almost an altered state of consciousness, after which I could not wait to get the room emptied. Suddenly it occurred to me what I was doing; as I dismantled the room, I was also stripping away an old identity, one that I had cherished but was now ready to let go. Evelyn Underhill would have known how I felt as I lugged black plastic bags of trash out of my office and found homes for unwanted books. I think she would have understood that it was as much a spiritual exercise as plain hard work.

> All those who have felt themselves urged towards the attainment of this transcendental vision have found that possessions interrupt the view; that claims, desires, attachments become centres of conflicting interest in the mind. They assume a false air of importance,

force themselves upon the attention, and complicate life. Hence, in the interest of self-simplification, they must be cleared away: a removal which involves for the real enthusiast little more sacrifice than the weekly visit of the dustman.[4]

One of the gifts of a retreat in a monastery or convent is that of a radically simplified environment—a bed, a desk, a chair, a lamp, a crucifix or an icon, and some pegs on which to hang a few clothes. There is a sufficiency, but nothing extra. I need fear no fragile decorative objects, filling all the surfaces. Motels too can offer a somewhat simplified space, but as someone who rarely watches television, I cannot resist the temptation to play with the remote control, continuing to flip through the channels even when nothing of interest comes to the screen.

I do not suggest that we should lead comfortless lives, sleeping on bare floors and eating beans straight from the can, but there is something vastly clarifying and liberating by taking stock of our surroundings now and then and asking, "Do my material possessions sustain me or burden me? What is there in the space around me that is crying out to be discarded?" It is a sign of our affluence that no matter how wealthy or poor we are, we are all choking on our possessions. This is not a problem in the so-called Third World, where sturdy cardboard boxes and plastic jugs are turned into household furnishings.

An occasional retreat is a wonderful way of resetting our spiritual clock and freeing ourselves, at least temporarily, from material excess. Ironically, a retreat is a relative luxury, requiring leisure to take a few days off and enough money for travel and the modest amount asked by most re-

---

4. *Mysticism*, 210-211.

ligious communities to maintain themselves. There is always the danger of romanticizing the experience, of playing at medieval piety and enduring austere bathrooms, secure in the knowledge that the austerity is only temporary.

～ Simplicity in Speech

As we can practice simplicity through the discipline of regularly clearing away the clutter of our possessions, we can also learn to simplify our speech. During World War II there were placards in public places reminding the careless: "Loose Lips Sink Ships." While it was doubtful that enemy agents were lurking in our Kansas City bus station or at the lunch counter in Woolworth's, most people lived with a new awareness that what they said might matter and that their words should therefore be uttered with care. Jesus commands the same caution, only in much stronger words: "I tell you, on the day of judgment you will have to give an account for every careless word you utter; for by your words you will be justified, and by your words you will be condemned" (Matthew 12:36–37). I had lived for decades without particularly noticing this admonition, which now I find terrifying. Language is one of the gifts that makes us human. How easy it is to accept that gift without thinking of the accompanying responsibility of good stewardship for its use!

Our words can inform. They can express feeling. They can convey beauty. They can obfuscate—a word I have never heard spoken, and most certainly a word that lives up to its meaning, for in ordinary conversation it might well confuse or make obscure what it should clarify. One of our family legends is about my cousin Denzil, who reputedly lost his job because his ornate and enormous vocabulary left his clients confused and a little frightened. I always enjoyed his company, but then from my earliest days I was addicted to words, which is perhaps why my new awareness of Jesus' admonition pulls me up short.

Jesus says, "Let your word be 'Yes, Yes' or 'No, No'; anything more than this comes from the evil one" (Matthew 5:37). Could he have anticipated an age when we hide behind specialized vocabularies and use words to conceal rather than to clarify? Each field—psychology, literature, philosophy, and theology—has its own arcane language to address the same great questions of meaning and experience. This is right and good so long as both intent and result are to clarify, but wasteful and wrong when the object is to conceal or exclude: "I know something you don't know; just try to figure it out." Sometimes during opaque lectures I imagine Jesus sitting in the audience, especially when he and his teachings are the object of discussion. When my daydream is especially vivid, he overturns the lectern and rips out the overhead projector, then tells us a story that even the children can understand.

In his novel *1984* George Orwell gave us the concept of doublethink, the simultaneous belief in two contradictory ideas. This is possible only when language is used perversely, to distract and to conceal the truth. He was writing at a time when governments and media used deceptively neutral language to conceal horrors, a practice still with us and growing steadily. Even when it is benevolent, bureaucratese obscures rather than enlightens. At best, it is a foolish waste; at worst, it sucks the life from our endeavor.

We become more honest, more nakedly ourselves, when we are able to say what we mean and mean what we say. We can simplify our speech by weaning ourselves from excessive use of qualifiers, those dull little words that allow us to escape responsibility for our utterances: *in my opinion, perhaps, maybe, somewhat, I may be all wrong but....* We can simplify our speech by becoming aware of empty chatter—our own and the chatter that surrounds us—and then rejecting its emptiness. The popularity of talk shows on radio and television is symptomatic of our time; instead of living, we talk or listen as others talk.

We grow in directness as we simplify our speech. Mastery of a familiar two-letter word can be a giant step toward spiritual health. To be able to say "No" without apology or excuse enables us to grow in true charity, for we avoid the trap of promising more than we can possibly deliver. It is all too easy to confuse mindless acquiescence with generosity. It does not mark us as self-centered when we are able to say plainly what we want, what we need, and what we fear. We merely stop playing guessing games with our friends and families. Perhaps most important of all, our prayers become honest.

⮑ Simplicity in Identity

Simplification of speech leads almost inevitably to stripping off the outer layers that obscure our true identity. For centuries the Hapsburg emperors were buried in the crypt of the Capuchin church in the heart of Vienna. According to the protocol, the pallbearers would knock at the door of the church and beg admission for the dead emperor. When asked who the corpse was, they would recite his royal titles one by one, only to be refused entrance after each. Finally, they would state his unadorned Christian name and be admitted. Birth and death are great levelers; on these thresholds we are stripped of pretense and defenses.

The church and academy, where I spend most of my time, abound in titles and hierarchy to an extent rivaling the Hapsburg. One of my Brooklyn friends delights in addressing letters to me as "The Reverend Professor Doctor Mother M. Guenther." That line fills the whole envelope and no doubt impresses our rural mailman! When I write letters to my clergy friends, I find myself checking my handy reference book: who is a Venerable, who is a Most Reverend, and who is merely a Reverend? There are analogies in the secular world, of course; only an expert in business protocol, for example, can decipher the pecking order of the various vice-presidents in a large corporation. Ultimately, though, we are like the dead emperor waiting outside the church door. I am convinced that God knows us on a first-name basis (if not by an embarrassing and irreverent nickname). Titles and uniforms can be useful in some circumstances, but it helps if we let both sit lightly upon us.

I was brought up to avoid the use of Christian names as disrespectful outside the most intimate circle. I can understand the formality of that time and place, but I am happy we have moved beyond it in many of our relationships. I want to know others and be known myself by a Christian name. It is my *given* name, chosen just for me, perhaps pondered long before my birth and—I suspect—the result of much family negotiation. (My father told me that he liked "Anneliese" but was outvoted by the New England side of the family.) So now, when I am asked, "What shall we call you?" I reply, "Margaret is fine. That's what God calls me."

So many components make up our identity—sex, family status, sexual orientation, work, nationality, race, physical appearance, political leanings. This list could go on and on, with each item contributing to the texture and richness of who we are. Ultimately, however, our identity in Christ is more than enough, and all that really matters. It would be quite sufficient if my friend in Brooklyn sent his letters to "Margaret, Child of God," although I am sure that it would create much confusion at the United States Postal Service.

~ Simplicity in Time

We can also live more simply in relation to time. A few years ago I succumbed to pressure from the outside world and got a fax machine in Jenkins Hollow. Jarringly out of place in the bare little room under the stairs, it is rarely called upon to perform. Yet every time I pass it, it reminds me of our modern obsession with time. We demand instant communication, and, absurdly, we think that it matters. That time might elapse, uncontrolled by us, is an alarming thought.

An outward and visible sign is the clocks that have proliferated in our homes. When I was a child we had one clock, which my grandfather wound every evening. My father had a pocket watch, and for my seventh birthday I received a Mickey Mouse watch. Now I live with the kitchen clock, the alarm clock, the travel clock, a handsome non-functioning clock won in a parish raffle, the clocks on the VCR, computer, and fax. If I had a microwave, there would be one there as well. The truly inescapable clock, however, is the one inside me, goading me on to keep up with the timetable. It is never off by more than a minute or two.

Our lives and our children's lives have become tightly scheduled to a degree unthinkable even a generation ago. While there may be occasional situations beyond our control, I suspect that many of us are also guilty of "obligation inflation," making sure that we are never quite done and that there is always one more thing looming just around the corner. God forbid that we should follow his example in creation: behold what we have done, pronounce it at least good enough, and then stop for a day to rest and enjoy it!

A long time ago I taught at a university where most of my students were Jewish. I found myself almost envious when they told me about their sabbath, with good food prepared ahead of time and then a day of deliberate rest.

Unlike my childhood memories of starchy Sunday afternoons, of sitting quietly in my scratchy "good" clothes while the grownups talked, the sabbath described by my students sounded like something to look forward to. Time is always a gift, but observance of the sabbath (which can come on any day of the week, an important point to remember for those of us who must work on Sunday) is a powerful reminder that God has given us this gift and expects us to use it, indeed enjoy it for itself.

If we cannot manage a full twenty-four hours, we can at least cultivate the habit of building little sabbaths into our crowded days. We can teach ourselves the art of prayerfully and re-creatively wasting time. Most of us are already able to waste considerable time joylessly and unintentionally. We leave the television on for another half-hour after our favorite program is over. We procrastinate when faced with boring little tasks. We read more of the newspaper than we need: does it really matter to me what the weather will be like in Berlin today, or what specials are being offered at the grocery store where I never shop? Some of us even dawdle over breakfast as we study the back of the cereal box.

On the other hand, the deliberate wasting of time by doing nothing can be an important spiritual discipline, especially if it is done with joy and in the spirit of re-creation. We may feel guilty and definitely out of step since everyone else looks so purposeful and busy. Yet a little holy time-wasting can create a bit of true sabbath—fifteen minutes, an hour, even half a day. We can rejoice in God's gift of time as we slow down to savor it.

～ Simplicity in Prayer

Finally, we can seek simplicity in our prayer. Structuring our days around prayer can provide a defense against the creeping clutter that crowds the hours and deadens the spirit. This is obviously easier for members of religious communities who gather regularly for corporate prayer, and more difficult for ordinary folk "in the world": for the mother of a young child or a worker holding two jobs, it is a luxury to stop everything for regular times of prayer. Just mumbling an adult equivalent of "Now I lay me down to sleep" before bed may feel like an achievement. Nevertheless, it *is* possible to observe the traditional times of prayer—morning, noon, evening, and night—so long as we remember that more is not necessarily better and that our prayer can be very brief. It is a matter of re-membering who we are, joined and knit together in the body of Christ. In those few moments we touch base, as it were, so that the rest of the day makes sense.

In these times of prayer throughout the day we can pray alone, or with family and friends. We can pray from a book, using something like the Daily Devotions for Individuals and Families in *The Book of Common Prayer* (BCP 137-140). Or we can pray without a book, simply punctuating the day with a bit of silence, a spontaneous verbal prayer, or the Lord's Prayer. The angelus, prayed morning, noon, and evening, reminds us of the wonder of the incarnation, that God chose and continues to choose to share our human life. However we may manage it, to build our day around prayer both simplifies and deepens our experience of time. Living in awareness of God's presence, we know a heightened sensitivity to God's world, both in its beauty and its woundedness.

The prayer book reminds us that the service of God is "perfect freedom" (BCP 57); thus, building our day on a foundation of prayer should set us free, not burden us with yet another task. It goes against much of our training to let our prayer sit lightly, even casually, upon us. Increasingly,

though, I am convinced that prayer is not so much something we *do* or *say* as how we *are*—grateful, questioning,
penitent, comfortable, adoring, sometimes listening carefully, sometimes silently companionable. But always open
and attentive. Always in conversation. We can get so tangled up in our devotional patterns—our idea of what we
should be doing and how we should be praying—that we
forget what we are about. We can forget the LORD'S injunction to "be still and know that I am God." From time to
time, we need to stop and savor the stillness.

Letting ourselves rest in silence is the ultimate simplification and, at the same time, is the most difficult kind of
prayer for many of us. We live in a society that floods us
with words and images, many of them beautiful, interesting, and valuable. It is hard to let go of them, even for a little while. Occasionally, I look at my bookshelves and ask
myself, "Would I be closer to God without so many books,
so many words?" The desert fathers thought so and abandoned even their holy books as distractions. I am not ready
for so drastic a step toward total simplicity, but as a child of
this culture know that I need constant reminders that God
is to be found in silence and solitude:

> Now there was a great wind, so strong that it was split-
> ting mountains and breaking rocks in pieces before the
> LORD, but the LORD was not in the wind; and after the
> wind an earthquake, but the LORD was not in the earth-
> quake; and after the earthquake a fire, but the LORD was
> not in the fire; and after the fire a sound of sheer silence.
> (1 Kings 19:11-12)

Again and again, scripture reminds us of the power of being alone in the silence—Elijah standing at the mouth of the
cave, Jesus driven by the Spirit into the harsh solitude of
the desert, Jesus again and again turning his back on the

multitudes to "go apart" to pray. Our lives can become so crowded—so filled with the good, the bad, and the trivial—that we cannot hear God's whisper. It helps to cultivate the prayer of listening.

〜 The Fruit of Simplicity

Just as our charity increases as we find our place in the Christian community, so too do we grow in generosity as we embrace simplicity. We are able to hold all things lightly and, if need be, let them go—our possessions, our money, our pretensions, even our anger, our prejudices, and our fears. But the letting-go, if it is the fruit of generous simplicity, can never be coerced. It must be joyful, and it must be voluntary. It is not to be confused with spiritual deadness, living without passion. Indeed, we live more passionately because we are set free from the burdensome work of holding on tightly to anything that comes within our grasp.

Flawed creatures that we are, we will never get it quite right, but we can keep practicing. I can let go of some things almost effortlessly, rather like the giveaway checker games of my childhood. I even find myself wishing that I liked elegant clothes and jewelry so that I could give them up. But then I hit a hard place after a period of easy letting-go—surely not my grandmother's piano, even though I rarely have time to play? And surely not the books, even the ponderous ones I know that I will never read again? Which simply proves that I am not St. Francis. (But after all, he did carry things to extremes.) Even if we cannot achieve a Franciscan ease of detachment, we can live more intentionally, savoring the intrinsic beauty of simplicity. We can rejoice in clean lines and solid materials, both literal and spiritual. We are wary of curlicues that distort and cheapen. We know when we have enough.

The value of simplicity came home to me powerfully last year when I was allowed to watch an artist put the finishing touches on a painting. A tiny dab of paint here, another tiny dab there, and Beth stood back. "I think it's time to kill the artist," she said. For a moment I was taken aback, since she is a gentle woman who seems unlikely to countenance the killing of anything. Then I understood what she meant: she knew the temptation to elaborate, but she also knew when it was time to let go. I remember her with gratitude when I find myself muttering to myself, "Time to kill the artist. Let go."

Jesus said to Martha, "You are worried and distracted by many things; there is need of only one thing" (Luke 10:41-42). There is some Martha in all of us. I know that I must fight the impulse to contend, "Yes, but...." After all, we *do* have need of only one thing. When we recognize it, as the Shakers remind us, we will "find ourselves in the place just right, 'Twill be in the Valley of Love and Delight."[5]

---

5. *The Shakers*, 295.

~ Chapter Nine

Praying Through Desolation

Why Have You Forsaken Me?

I have a hard time with Good Friday. Every year I think, "If I were God, I would do this differently." When I let myself be vulnerable to the sights and sounds of the crucifixion, it is too much. Too much cruelty. Too much exposure. Too much pain. There is altogether too much suffering at Golgotha: the suffering of a tortured body, never to be underestimated, for we are our bodies. Then there is the suffering of betrayal—not just the crass betrayal by Judas, but also the passive betrayal of the melting away of his trusted friends. There is also the suffering of waste and failure. All that has gone before—healing, preaching, teaching, friendship—seems now without purpose.

So much suffering would be bearable, even meaningful, if Jesus had sensed God's loving presence. Yet as he hung on the cross, he cried out, "My God, my God, why have you forsaken me?" Matthew tells us that he still had strength to "cry with a loud voice." I am haunted by that cry. Was it a shout of anger at yet another betrayal or the involuntary scream of a tortured man? Defiant shout or piteous scream, Jesus' words were a prayer, the prayer of the abandoned.

To be forsaken by God is to be abandoned to meaninglessness; it is a great mystery that feels like punishment or a cruel joke. How can it be that those of us who love God and who have been taught from infancy that God loves us experience such depths of despair? The pain of being forsaken surpasses and swallows up all other pain. When we feel abandoned—whether we are an infant crying alone in a crib or a nursing home resident enduring an endless, sleepless night—memory does not help. The memory of the warmth and safety of a mother's arms, the memory of bright and fruitful younger days can seem like taunts, adding to the anguish. Time stands still. There is no future. The present is endless and excruciating. The only prayer is an anguished, "Why?"

We live our own crucifixions. Sometimes they are tiny: patches of desolation that are genuine enough but easily forgotten once they are past. At other times they are overwhelming: sorrow heaped upon sorrow, until our desolation appears endless and total. Whatever the degree, inevitably in the spiritual life there come times when God seems remote, inattentive, perhaps not there at all. Our suffering may be acute, but more often we merely feel spiritually leaden. Our prayer is mechanical and pointless. We remember, at least theoretically, that we are made in God's image, that God loves us, and that God knows us intimately, indeed that the very hairs of our head are numbered. But where has the warm glow gone? It does not seem fair that our faithfulness is not rewarded, so that we find ourselves out in the cold. God has become an abstraction, an elegant hypothesis, but scarcely the source or object of ardent love. After the peaks and valleys of intense religious experience, we are stranded on a plateau. Or perhaps mired in a swamp, or slowly drying out in the desert.

The language of the Christian tradition offers impressive terms for this state of spiritual discomfort: instead of consolation, we are experiencing desolation; instead of sweetness in prayer, aridity. "Desolation" and "aridity" are hard words and in this context have a medieval or monastic aura. I might say to my Benedictine spiritual director, "I could certainly use a little consolation right now," and he would know that I yearned for more than a kindly pat and a "there, there." But most of the time I would articulate my malaise less elegantly: I am stuck. I am just going through the motions. I have the spiritual blahs. I say the right things at the right time, but I am not at all sure that anybody is listening. God may be mad at me; at least, he is not speaking to me. I know the words but not the music—at least, I am not hearing any music. In other words, God is silent. I am on hold. There is not even a reassuring recorded message: "Your call is important to us; please wait for the next available operator." There is nothing to do but to wait.

~ Waiting on God

Waiting in the midst of desolation and aridity is an essential theme in many of the psalms, the prayers of a people trying to pray faithfully and honestly: "For God alone my soul in silence waits; from him comes my salvation" (Psalm 62:1). This kind of waiting is serious business, Indeed, it is a matter of life and death, for God, our salvation, is our only source of safety. To wait on God in our own humble silence, enfolded in the mysterious silence of God, is lonely work, especially when it feels as if everyone around us is confident of God's loving presence.

Such waiting, indeed any waiting, goes against our grain. Maybe it was easier for the people of ancient Israel, but we in the industrialized west are a time-obsessed people, nervous of too much open-endedness and edgy at the prospect of "empty" time. Like newborns, who feel safest when they are snugly swaddled, most of us like the security of a predictable timetable. We surround ourselves with reminders of the press of time. I have not yet succumbed to a tiny, hand-held computer to manage my schedule, but I cling to my little black pocket-sized book like a lifeline. When it was briefly lost, dropped by the curb as I climbed out of a taxi, I had a moment of panic: I might have to drop out of life if I did not know where I had to be when. We live in a world in which it is nearly impossible to escape the implicit command to keep moving, to do *something*. Time, after all, is money. Time spent waiting is wasted time.

Yet there are times in the life of prayer when we can do nothing more than wait upon God. Sometimes these are times of crisis, despair, and desolation, but often they are ordinary times when the old ways no longer work, and we find ourselves "in a barren and dry land where there is no water" (Psalm 63:1). It is a lonely place. Our only recourse is faithful waiting.

Waiting rooms of all sorts are for me powerful icons of the prayerful work of waiting. Whether they are hospital waiting rooms with uncomfortable plastic chairs and wastebaskets overflowing with discarded newspapers and styrofoam coffee cups, the dentist's reception room with its admonitory posters on tooth care and its odd assortment of tattered magazines, or any airport—since they all look remarkably alike—I am always reminded of the barrenness and apparent aridity of waiting on God. I say "apparent" because, while the hours spent in airports (where I routinely show up too early) are certainly barren and tedious, waiting on God is necessary and ultimately fruitful.

Even the most ordinary waiting is never easy. It calls for a kind of surrender, a letting-go. I may pace the floor of the airport lounge, fuss and fume inwardly at my tardy dentist, read the paperback book brought along for just such eventualities, but ultimately there is nothing to do but to wait. When we wait, we relinquish control. It (whatever "it" is) happens when it happens. It comes when it comes. Even when we know that it *must* come—whether it is the birth of a child, the flattening of the line on the monitor when physical life finally ends, or the belated boarding call for the plane.

But prayerful waiting is no ordinary barren helplessness: here our soul is waiting for God. Even if it be grudging, our surrender, along with our awareness of our own powerlessness, is inevitable. This should be self-evident, but I need constant reminders. Again and again I must discover, always with some surprise, that God is in charge and that I am not God. I cannot capture God, trap God, somehow secure God either by my wiles or—more likely in our driven society—by my hard work, efficiency, and general competence. God's silence is a potent reminder of my smallness. It is all too easy to see myself as God's capable administrative assistant, the invaluable link in the chain of command, the one person who really knows what is going on. The CEO, after all, seems oblivious of organization and lacking in management skills.

We want our prayer to *work*. We want to know that we have got it right and that our words have been heard. Unstructured, seemingly ineffective time in prayer, time when "nothing happens," makes us uneasy. It is tempting to make our prayer into a production instead of a way of being, an ongoing stance of openness and receptivity. Products, after all, can be regulated. They do not grow naturally but are turned out, and we can produce more if we work longer hours or if we diminish the quality of the product. It is absurd and a little frightening to imagine our life in Christ on a factory model—revise and maximize that rule of life, find the most efficient way of praying, and then pray faster.

Fruitfulness is another matter. To come to fruition demands the passage of seemingly empty time and simply letting be. The process is oblivious of our compulsion to get things done, to get the job over with, and to chalk up results. It still takes nine months to create a baby. Plants still need sun, rain, soil, and time to grow. Typically dull brown and bare, a fallow field does not impress us with its majesty or beauty. Fallow time, the waiting time in prayer, is also dull and bare; but it is not wasted time even though it seems that way.

Even as I write of the goodness of fallow time and the inevitable experience of the silence of God, I confess my own lack of understanding. In my more grandiloquent moments, when I forget my place in God's great economy, I catch myself offering suggestions for better and easier ways of faithful living. Why make it so hard? Once God has our attention and we realize that our yearning for God is at the heart of all our yearning, isn't that enough? Why can't we not bask unperturbed in the knowledge of God's love?

∽ The Dark Night

The times of silence, which can seem like failure, are really threshold times of testing. Tests are rarely pleasurable, and they can be difficult, strenuous, even excruciatingly painful. But they always have a purpose. In my university teaching days I always had to remind my students—and myself—that tests were not the final exams. Rather, they were a device for checking progress along the way, to find gaps and deficiencies, to consolidate and ultimately to strengthen. Good tests, even when the results were disastrous, pointed toward eventual good news.

Testing always has a purpose. It is not the same as toying with someone, teasing or tormenting. Given my druthers, I would rather not be tested, but untested I remain an unknown quantity, a matter of appearances only. Serious tests can push us to our limit, bring us to the edge of despair when we are sure that we are not strong enough, when we feel that we will be destroyed. Serious tests, when they are past, leave us surprised, fatigued, and perhaps a bit shaken, but amazed at the new depths we have found within ourselves. The God who loves us tests us by being silent.

An untested faith, like an untested miracle drug or an untested fire extinguisher, is full of promise but not yet dependable enough to be trusted. Falling in love is a wondrous experience, but it is not yet love; rather it is a prelude to love, a necessary preliminary. We fall in love with prospective mates and partners, we fall in love with our newborn babies, and we fall in love with God. Yet love requires time to be deeply rooted, both in our human relationships and in our intimate relationship with God. Growing up spiritually can be a laborious process, just as our physical and intellectual growth is accomplished in slow and gradual stages. Paul says as much to the impatient Corinthians:

> And so, brothers and sisters, I could not speak to you as spiritual people, but rather as people of the flesh, as infants in Christ. I fed you with milk, not solid food, for you were not ready for solid food. Even now you are still not ready, for you are still of the flesh. (1 Corinthians 3:1–3a)

John of the Cross, the sixteenth-century Spanish Carmelite mystic and poet, uses the same imagery to explain

the significance of the "dark night" of the soul, the lonely
state when God seems to have withdrawn his presence and
favor. Speaking of the need for the enthusiastic beginner to
be rid of imperfections, John writes:

> [God] does this by introducing them [those in the begin-
> ner's state] into the dark night.... There, through pure
> dryness and interior darkness, He weans them from the
> breasts of these gratifications and delights, takes away
> all these trivialities and childish ways, and makes them
> acquire virtues by very different means. No matter how
> earnestly beginners in all their actions and passions
> practice the mortification of self, they will never be able
> to do it entirely—far from it—until God accomplishes it
> in them passively by means of the purgation of this
> night.[1]

John's use of the metaphor of weaning implies that this
seemingly harsh treatment is really a sign of divine favor,
even when it is experienced as a painful abandonment.
John repeats the metaphor of moving from milk to solid
food in his description of a maternal God who removes the
soul's baby clothes and puts it down from his arms so that
it is forced to walk alone. Deprived of the "delicate and
sweet food of infants," it learns to eat bread with crust.[2]
This is a demanding love, challenging us to embrace maturity.

In the psalms, the dark time of waiting is not in vain,
even when God is hidden and silent. This is the *deus abscon-
ditus* of the mystical tradition, the God who has absconded,
run off, and abandoned the faithful. Yet the abandonment

---

1. John of the Cross, *Selected Writings*, ed. Kieran Kavanaugh, OCD (New
   York: Paulist Press, 1987), 178.
2. *Ibid.*, 189.

is only apparent: "I waited patiently upon the LORD; he stooped to me and heard my cry" (Psalm 40:1). "Patiently" is the key word in this verse. Patient waiting is purposeful. Patience is a chosen stance, a deliberate and thoughtful surrender based on hope. It is a not an easy virtue, if indeed any virtues thrive in us effortlessly. Ironically, patience is another name for solitaire, the mechanical, repetitive card game that I find almost hypnotic, especially when the computer version of the game spares me even the task of shuffling the cards. By contrast, the patience of the waiting soul is alive and expectant: this is especially apparent in the Latin version of Psalm 40, which begins, *Expectans, expectavi*—"expectantly, I expected." Yet suffering is also at the heart of the word, for to be patient is to suffer, to endure. Just as a hospital patient necessarily and usually voluntarily relinquishes control in the hope of healing, so the waiting soul accepts—by no means easily—the bleakness of spiritually arid times or the painful state of desolation.

～ Praying in Times of Trial

The arid times come to all. These fallow periods in prayer, when we go through the motions and struggle to remain faithful, are different from the times of true desolation, when we search for excuses for God, perhaps let ourselves be angry with God, or even doubt God's existence. Often these times coincide with genuine tribulation and suffering—illness, loss, and gratuitously inflicted cruelty. John of the Cross, for example, experienced the dark night when he was imprisoned, starved, and brutally maltreated by his fellow friars. He did not, however, see the harsh circumstances of his life as the cause of his profound despair, but rather as a parallel experience, less significant but somehow an external manifestation of his spiritual suffering.

Rejection and persecution by members of his order, painful as that might be, was nothing compared to excruciating dread that God had indeed abandoned him. To abandon, after all, is to depart without any intention of returning. The psalmist says, "My eyes have failed from watching for your promise, and I say, 'When will you comfort me?'" (Psalm 119:82). From the cross, while suffering physical torment, Jesus quoted another psalm of spiritual anguish: "My God, my God, why have you forsaken me?" (Psalm 22:1). We do not know the words and thoughts of Mary and the other faithful women who watched at the foot of the cross, but they too must have experienced the coincidence of great tribulation—for the pain of helplessly watching a beloved person suffer is in its way as great as the pain of the loved one—along with a devastating sense of God's withdrawal.

How can we pray when everything seems hopeless, when sickness and death threaten to overwhelm us, and our suffering seems unjust and pointless? If we live long enough, even those of us who would shrink from claiming the mystical gifts of John of the Cross or hesitate to compare our own pain to the suffering of Jesus on the cross know these times. We may need to pray for ourselves or for others, but true prayer in such times is never easy. It can feel like a wrestling match—"God, whoever you are and if you are listening at all, how can you do this? Do you really think you can get away with this?" Or it can be a bargaining session—"Just let this pass, and I'll be good forever."

We might even go so far as to offer ourselves as a substitute for someone we love. A few years ago, my newborn grandson suffered a series of frightening episodes in his first week: he simply stopped breathing. As I sat on a plane, trying to absorb the medical reports and wondering whether this brand new life might be shortened or impaired by a neurological accident, I found myself almost unconsciously muttering, "Take me instead." Almost at once I panicked: did I really mean it? Was I trying to cut a deal with God, offering my aging body to a stroke or a heart attack in exchange for a baby's health? For the rest of the flight, I gravitated: "Yes, you mean it. No, you're being dramatic. Maybe you should start praying that God didn't hear you or at least that he won't take you seriously. Or that he will say something like, 'It's the thought that counts.'" Fortunately I never had to face that time of trial; as of this writing, he is a delightful, robust little boy unmarked by his stressful first days.

I am nervous of being prescriptive about how to pray when circumstances threaten to crush us and God seems unreliable, if not totally absent. Alone in the darkness and in pain, with the psalmist I want to cry out, "My grief is this: the right hand of the Most High has lost its power" (77:10). These are the times when going through the motions of prayer is important, even though it seems mechanical and fruitless. Structures help sustain us; their very lifelessness makes no demands on us and calls for no real investment of spiritual energy, which in times of desolation we simply do not have. Repetitive prayers, those prayers known from childhood or memorized through frequent use, can hold us together when we are on the brink of falling apart.

These times when the right hand of God seems to have lost its power are also times for candid spontaneous prayer, which may bear little resemblance to our normally polite, liturgical conversations with God. I rely heavily on the psalms in times of desolation: they could never be accused of politeness, a quality esteemed by many Anglicans but not numbered among the officially recognized virtues. Speaking raw truth from the depths, the psalms beg, question, and complain. They even rage. They make it clear that we need not go gently into the night, and that God will not destroy us.

There may be times, however, when we cannot pray, even mechanically. Perhaps we are too angry with God to articulate our rage. Perhaps we have lost hope. Perhaps our pain—physical, emotional, or spiritual—is so intense that we are not capable of thought or speech. These are the times when we rely on the prayers of others. However isolated we might feel—and our sense of isolation might be total—we can let ourselves be held by the community.

Daily we pray, "Save us from the time of trial," which seems to me a much more useful prayer than "Lead us not into temptation." Maybe it is a sign of age, but I can deal with the more common temptations. Trial is quite another matter: I do not know how strong I am. I have some idea of how strong I *should* be, but it is dangerous to be too confident until my convictions have been tested.

With great humility I read the stories of Christian martyrs: not the flamboyant and often apocryphal accounts of the sufferings of medieval saints, but those martyr-witnesses of our own time who endured the darkness and refused to let it overcome them, who ultimately found themselves suffused with God's love in the midst their desolation. Dietrich Bonhoeffer, Edith Stein, Corrie ten Boom, Janani Luwum, and in more recent times such martyr-witnesses as hostages Terry Waite and Terry Anderson, all give us glimpses of spiritual endurance. I doubt that any one of them would profess any special holiness or claim to be a "mystic." Possibly they surprised even themselves.

So we pray "Save us from the time of trial" and hope that our prayer will be answered. But we cannot be sure and indeed have no right to expect immunity from affliction. Nor can we anticipate how we might react to our world collapsing around us, relentless pain, or catastrophic loss. There are some prayers that we cannot practice in advance. A few years ago, when airplane hijackings were too common for comfort, I would play with a fantasy as I sat buckled in my seat tens of thousands of feet in the air. It was a sort of test: would I offer myself sacrificially to the hijacker to be thrown out of the plane or shot, bravely proclaiming, "Take me, I'm a priest"? Or to get down to basics, "Take me, I'm a Christian"? Or would I cower in my seat and beg for mercy, "Please, young man, I'm just a grandmother"? I know how I would like the scenario to unfold, but I could never be sure.

More to the point, in that thin, threshold time just before dawn when God can seem sometimes very near and sometimes hidden, I ponder how I will face the inevitable physical and quite probable mental diminishment that comes with age. What would my prayers be like if I were bedfast and incontinent, completely dependent on the care of others? What will my prayer be at the moment of my death? To what extent is my faith strong because my body is strong and my days are predictable and comfortable? In other words, how will I fare in the time of ultimate trial? As in my airplane fantasy, I cannot know the answer. Little times of pain and powerlessness can be spiritual fire drills or Lamaze classes preparing for the second great passage, useful but ultimately nothing like the real thing. I can only hope.

～ Deliver Us from Evil

Even as we pray to be spared the time of trial, we plead also to be delivered from evil. I have great respect for evil and become uncomfortable when we trivialize and try to domesticate it, or even turn it into entertainment via mediocre movies and television specials. Evil is definitely with us and difficult to define, but I certainly know it when I have got a whiff of it. Put most simply, it is manifested in consistent, conscious choices made in diametrical opposition to the God of love.

Where is God when evil seems to triumph? How can we pray, indeed *what* can we pray when God seems not merely absent, but powerless or even nonexistent? Theologians have struggled with these questions for centuries, but there are no neat, palatable answers. Theodicy, the imposing name given to that field of theological endeavor seeking to defend God's goodness in the face of evil, keeps scholars busy but, for me at least, their theological formulas fail to convince. Ultimately, we are left with Job, baffled yet willing to let God be God:

> I know that you can do all things,
> and that no purpose of yours can be thwarted....
> I had heard of you by the hearing of the ear,
> but now my eye sees you;
> therefore I despise myself,
> and repent in dust and ashes. (Job 42:2, 5-6)

Resigning ourselves to penitence in dust and ashes seems like an easy out, however. The question of evil will not go away that simply. We are supposed to be praying and, quite possibly, wrestling as well. Wrestling with the question, wrestling with our doubts, and wrestling with God.

It is important to distinguish between evil and sin. Despite all our good intentions, sin is inescapable; as Paul writes in his letter to the Romans, "All have sinned and fall short of the glory of God" (3:23). He might have added, "And will undoubtedly sin again." In a similar vein later in the letter, he laments his own propensity for going astray: "I do not understand my own actions. For I do not do what I want, but I do the very thing I hate" (7:15). Yet our sins can be repented and absolved. The cold willfulness of evil is another matter. Evil, whether in the actions of an individual or in the behavior of whole nations, is a challenge to our prayer. How, we wonder, can the all-powerful, all-loving God permit the horror of the Holocaust, the suffering of children, and the widespread and increasing official use of torture?

How can we pray when we have glimpsed evil, when we know it is there but we cannot quite get hold of it? Sometimes it is subtle and insidious, so familiar a part of our lives that its presence is taken for granted. Then our complicity is passive. Then it is easy to deny its existence and, like the priest and the Levite in the parable of the Good Samaritan, pass by on the other side, convinced that what we have seen has nothing to do with us. So I cajole myself with the rationalization that I have not personally oppressed people of color; indeed, I have always treated them with respect and friendliness and taught my children to do likewise. Surely the evil of racism has nothing to do with me! Maybe evil is too strong a word for what is merely a pervasive "problem" that will go away on its own if we just give it time.

Often the evil is geographically or socially far removed from us. If we avert our eyes, we can live in ignorance for long periods. There is self-interest in such denial; we cannot face the reality that the fabric is very thin, and that no one is safe. It is possible to disregard institutionalized evil if we are able to convince ourselves that it is not happening to "people like us" (we think) or that perhaps reports are exaggerated.

Even if our encounters with true evil are rare, it is inevitable that we confront the dark underside of contemporary society. Despite years spent in urban ministry, I am profoundly aware of the limitation of my own vision. I have been sheltered throughout my life; I have never been in genuine want, and I have never been exposed to physical violence. Yet I cannot read the daily newspaper or watch the evening news without being brought into stark awareness of the violence and cruelty that surround even the most protected. My mind is filled with these images and stories from the media: emaciated children in African refugee camps, tourists gunned down as they visit the pyramids, ruthless slaughter in the name of "ethnic cleansing," wartime atrocities of half-century ago finally disclosed. Is there no end to the awareness that is thrust upon us? Closer to home, almost every day brings stories of children horribly maltreated and even killed by those closest to them, the very people who should be their protectors.

It is crucial that we pray for these people whom we will never see, for the victims and for the perpetrators. We can group our intercessions by categories—the hungry, the huddled refugees, those unjustly imprisoned, those undergoing torture, the abused children—simply naming them before God and waiting with them in silence. When we can, it is helpful to be specific. One abused child, prayed for by name, can make all maltreated children come alive for us. The picture of a malnourished Rwandan refugee can be a vivid reminder of all the displaced and hopeless. (One of my friends keeps a scrapbook of pictures from newspapers and magazines to help him as he prays his intercessions. It is loose-leaf, so that it can be updated regularly.) If we know the name and story of one person persecuted for her beliefs, we can let her represent all those unjustly imprisoned. For months I breathed a little prayer for Jewish dissident Nathan Sharansky, imprisoned by the Soviets for his beliefs. I knew virtually nothing about him, but his name and the days he had served were posted in the yard of a synagogue that I passed regularly on my way to church.

It is also crucial that we struggle in prayer with issues of injustice and oppression, especially when they seem not to affect us directly. The big question, of course, is this: how do I pray in such a way that my prayer is not merely a pious exercise? How do I deal with the tension between forms and structures that have benefitted me and the damaging consequences of these economic and political systems to others? One of the blessings of our Anglican way is our openness to ambiguity and our resistance to simplistic answers. Our life of prayer, to say nothing of our day-to-day existence, would be easier if we could close our eyes to the complexity of our world. Corporate sin, including our own accountability, is always difficult to pin down, understand, and handle. It is tempting to go to extremes: to close our minds and hearts or to castigate ourselves theatrically, hoping that extravagant language of repentance will suffice and that we will not have to change in any painful way. To live prayerfully with ambiguity is much harder, at least in part because our work is never done.

Here it is essential to combine our prayer with action. Not everyone is called to activism (which may or may not be helpful in bringing peace and justice to a particular region or group), but we can strive to link our prayer with our daily life. How or whether we vote is a political action, but it is also reflective of our desire to do God's will. We can offer our time and money as a sign of our commitment to God's work. What is perhaps most difficult, however, is our commitment to witness, to speak out when it would be much easier to remain silent. Quite literally, after all, a witness is a martyr. This is not a path to be chosen lightly, even when it does not lead to a painful death.

Heterosexuals can witness by their refusal to tolerate homophobic jokes and put-downs. Christians can witness by their opposition to anti–Semitic actions and policies. White people can witness by their confrontation of racial slurs, and black people can do likewise. The privileged can witness by insisting on the dignity of the dispossessed. If we are able to act out our prayers for love and justice, rather than consigning them to some spiritual attic of abstraction, we will have gained relatively easy admission to the noble army of martyrs. Which is not to say that it will be all that easy! When God is silent as we wrestle with the complexity of life at the edge of the millennium, when we struggle to match our prayers with our deeds, we are being pushed toward spiritual adulthood. To use the imagery of John of the Cross, the soft, sweet food is gone, and we are left alone to chew on bread with crusts. It is time for us to grow up.

⤳ It Will Be All Right

One of my favorite stories about living through dark and difficult times is Matthew's account of the disciples, alone in their boat and tossed by the winds (14:22-33). After feeding the multitude, Jesus made his disciples set out across the lake in the boat, leaving him behind. I wonder if they felt abandoned, if they wished that he would come with them or perhaps let them stay with him. "Why," they might have asked, "must we be left on our own? Why can't we always stay close to you?"

I ask this question every year at the feast of the Ascension, which always feels to me more like the feast of the Abandonment. Why should we be asked to celebrate being left on our own? Why should we be made to get into that boat when we would rather wait on the shore, even if we cannot go up into the hills with him? Could it be that Jesus is saying, "Trust yourself. Don't cling. You will be surprised at what you can do. And I won't be far away, and I won't be gone for long. You won't be really alone."

Jesus takes his time. The disciples are far from shore, and the boat is buffeted all night by the wind and the waves. It is almost dawn when he comes to them. Any night spent in watching is long and dark, but the men in the boat must also have been filled with fear. They are far from land, struggling against the wind and beaten by waves. Is the boat large enough, strong enough?

Fear is fed by uncertainty: how is this going to turn out? Can we believe the assurance that "weeping may spend the night, but joy comes in the morning" (Psalm 30:6)? Will joy come in the morning? And for that matter, will morning ever come? The dark night of the soul is aptly named. The disciples in that stormy night undoubtedly recalled times of intimacy with Jesus, ordinary times of shared meals and conversation and numinous times when they were power-fully aware of God's love. But that is *memory*. The present is bleak, without hope, without any conviction that the night will have an end. They were experiencing a collective dark night.

Then Jesus comes to them—and they do not recognize him. Matthew tells us that they are terrified and cry out with fear. In my imagination I have been with the fright-ened disciples more than once. I must learn again and again that he does not come in the way or the appearance that we expect. That he comes walking on the surface of the water captures our attention: not because we seek to understand the whys and wherefores of the reversal of the natural or-der, but because the significance lies in the unlikeliness, the unexpectedness of his appearance. The disciples are not looking for him to come walking on the water. Their vision of the possibilities is limited.

The gospels tell us of other instances when the disciples failed to recognize Jesus, most of them associated with the risen Christ rather than the human Teacher. On the road to Emmaus, his friends walk and talk with him, and recognize him only over a shared meal (Luke 24:13-35). Mary Magdalene stoops to look into the empty tomb, then mistakes him for the gardener (John 20:11-18). It seems part of the human condition to look in the wrong direction, fail to recognize who or what is before us, and then to be frightened of what we have seen but cannot understand.

In the story of Jesus walking on the water to the disciples in the boat, he says three things to them, which are to be taken to heart by all who find themselves adrift, buffeted by wind and wave, and far from shore. First, he tells them to *take heart*. Heart is at the root of word "courage," which is not foolhardiness, but steadfastness. Heart is needed if we are to face into the storm and into the unknown.

Second, *it is I*. Jesus identifies himself and makes it clear that the abandonment is only apparent. The disciples have not been forgotten; indeed, they have never really been alone. And yet their terror was real. We have to ask: was Jesus playing games with them? Some medieval writers thought so. The anonymous thirteenth-century author of *The Ancrene Riwle*, a book of instruction for three anchoresses, offers the picture of Jesus as mother, playing hide and seek with the childlike soul who seeks him:

> Our Lord, when he allows us to be tempted, is playing with us as a mother with her darling child. She runs away from him and hides, and leaves him on his own, and he looks around for her, calling "Mama! Mama!" and crying a little, and then she runs to him quickly, her arms outspread, and she puts them round him, and kisses him, and wipes his eyes. In the same way, our

Lord sometimes leaves us alone for a while and with-
draws his grace, comfort, and consolation.[3]

It is a delightful, yet at the same time troubling picture: the
game is fun only if both players know that it is a game.

Third, he told them to *have no fear.* Jesus repeats these
words countless times. Those times that God breaks into
human life are often heralded by this admonition. We need
to be reminded again and again that the opposite of love is
not hate but fear. Fear paralyzes. Fear stunts growth. Fear
keeps us from risk. Fear chokes creativity. Fear kills our
generosity. Fear leaves us cowering in the bottom of the
boat, thinking only of survival.

It is interesting to note that the storm is still raging
when Jesus says, "Have no fear." Even the reassurance of
his presence does not automatically make everything easy
or magically change the scene from one of danger to one of
serenity. Yet the cowering disciples—and we—are assured
that somehow, ultimately, we are safe. That it will be all
right.

The Roman Catholic theologian Margaret Hebblethwaite writes that she instinctively greeted her firstborn, seconds after his birth, with the words, "Dominic
Paul, it's all right, it's all right." Upon reflection, she observed that this "common message of comfort from a
mother to her child" is a metaphysical statement.[4] In these
instinctively murmured words of comfort, mothers do not
deny the pain, uncertainty, even the terror of life. They
simply remind the child—and themselves—that at the
deepest level, it truly is all right.

---

3. *The Ancrene Riwle,* tr. M. B. Salu (London: Burns & Oates, 1955), 134.
4. *Motherhood and God* (Wilton, CT: Morehouse Barlow, 1984), 31-33.

It is all right: these are such simple little words, words probably spoken by mothers as Herod's soldiers searched the houses of Bethlehem for baby boys, by mothers in boxcars en route to death camps, by mothers in all times and all places. Mary must have murmured these words to Jesus; perhaps, like Dominic Paul, these were the first words he heard. Every Good Friday I wonder anew if he felt their truth deep within when he let go and commended his spirit to his Father.

This is the great promise recorded by Julian of Norwich in her *Showings*. She lived in the fourteenth century, a time of plague, violence, social and political instability. It was a chaotic time not unlike ours, when people were adrift in the darkness, buffeted by wind and waves. She herself had known great physical suffering, receiving her visions when she was at the point of death. She also knew the terror of evil, for not all her visions were beatific: in her sleep she felt herself in the clutch of a hideous devil, whom she banished by keeping her eyes fixed on the cross. Ultimately, she knew that she was safe and that it was indeed "all right."

> On one occasion the good Lord said, "Everything is going to be all right." On another, "You will see for yourself that every sort of thing will be all right." He did not say, "You will not be troubled, you will not be belabored, you will not be disquieted," but he said: "You will not be overcome." God wants us to pay attention to these words and always to be strong in faithful trust, in well-being and in woe, for he loves us and delights in us, and so he wishes us to love him and delight in him and trust greatly in him, and all will be well.[5]

---

5. *Showings*, 315.

We are not promised that everything will be easy. We are not promised a rose garden, but that other garden of ominous darkness. But ultimately, it will be all right. We are working with a safety net. We are held and contained in the ultimate goodness of God's love. The night has its terrors, but the winds and waves will not destroy us.

Chapter Ten

Praying in Community

Who Are My Mother and My Brothers?

I remember an old *Peanuts* cartoon that shows Charlie Brown sitting in a box and looking glum, with a caption that read, "I love mankind; it's people I can't stand." Those of us who are members of the church might amend this to read, "I love God; it's the people sitting next to me I can't stand." Our sisters and brothers, the flawed and limited individuals who share the pew with us, tend to get in the way of our religious devotions. In its frequent wrongheadedness and frailty, the Christian community can seem like an impediment to our closeness to God. Prayer would be so much easier if it were a solo performance, with no one to distract or annoy us! The situation reminds me of a radio interview with a prison warden who remarked plaintively, "We aren't getting the same class inmates we used to."

In my years as a priest and as a seminary professor, I have heard again and again whenever the potential of a particular parish—large or small, urban, suburban, or rural—was discussed, "Well, yes, St. Matthew's has promise, but that's a parish with *real* problems." This would be said ruefully, suggesting that St. Matthew's might look all right to the casual observer, but it was in fact a sorry bunch of misguided people. Which it probably was. Conversations about parishes began to sound to me a lot like conversations about families or marriages: yes, there are some good relationships there and good intentions, but plenty of dysfunction or pathology or denial—whatever the current jargon of creeping negativity might be. It is as if we believe that somewhere a perfect Christian community exists, even as we dream that somewhere we could find a perfect marriage or a perfect family. In the meantime, we are stuck with the challenging imperfection of reality.

Paul's letters tell us that parishes have always been in trouble. The congregation in Corinth alone would give any struggling rector a headache: the Corinthians were divided in their loyalties, they had an exalted opinion of their own spiritual gifts, there was more than a little hanky-panky among parishioners, and they were stingy in their pledging. Paul, who loved them in spite of their shortcomings, concludes his second letter to them with an exhortation to clean up their act: "Put things in order, listen to my appeal, agree with one another, live in peace; and the God of love and peace will be with you" (2 Corinthians 13:11). The Corinthians sound suspiciously up-to-date; they would fit in nicely with any discussion of the problems at St. Matthew's.

Now and then, when I am in a rebellious mood and feeling like Charlie Brown in his box, I wonder: why do we come to church? What does God have to do with ushers and pledge cards and committees and vestries? What keeps us from worshiping God on our own? And for that matter, what *is* the church? What is the connection between flawed, struggling St. Matthew's and the mystical body of Christ? Faithful participation in any parish sooner or later reveals the very human limitations of its members—and its clergy. Perhaps that is why I enjoy a superb liturgy in a parish where I am a total stranger: I can keep my illusions of holy perfection. I do not need to know about vestry conflicts or clergy shortcomings, and I certainly do not have to concern myself with budgets and boilers. For a little while, I can bask in a pleasant liturgical haze.

The church, of course, is more than the local parish, more than our denomination, more than the Anglican Communion, more than the wild variety of faithful people living in our own time and calling themselves Christian. The church stretches back to the spoiled, difficult Corinthians, to the disciples who approached Jesus asking for the best seats in the kingdom of God, to the upper room where Jesus broke bread and shared wine with his friends. It extends to times and places remote from ours and to people very different from us. Triumphal at times and persecuted at times, clearly visionary and hopelessly wrongheaded, the earthly institution is an imperfect reflection of the true church, which does not exist in time or space.

We muddle on in the hope of one day getting it right, of living into the example of loving community modeled by Jesus when he knelt as a servant to wash the feet of his friends. Ironically, it is encouraging to remember that the congregation in the upper room was also far from perfect—Judas was a thief and a traitor, and Peter, the rock on whom Jesus promised to build his church, was frightened into denying his Teacher. The other disciples were not much better: they fled the city and hid in fear behind closed doors. Jesus must have known from the beginning that he was constructing his church—the *ecclesia*, the assembly of the faithful—with defective material, albeit the best available. He began with a group of ordinary, well-intentioned people, a community centered around him and bound together by their love for him. Not much has changed!

So we come to church. We may come for spurious or trivial reasons: in a recent newspaper article about a mega-parish, for example, one member explained his loyalty by saying, "I like being around successful people on Sundays." More commonly we might hear, "I like the music" or "I don't believe much myself, but it seems like a good thing for the children" or "I haven't been to church since I was a child; I thought I'd give it another try." However shallow and poorly motivated they might seem, such reasons are not to be discounted since they are among the myriad ways God hooks us and draws us into community. Hence too we should look kindly upon Christmas and Easter Christians, even when they sit in our favorite pew and make us feel crowded out on our own turf: God has got their attention, if only fleetingly. Sometimes that is all it takes; I call this the miracle of the hairline fracture.

We come to church because we hunger and thirst for something that we may be unable to articulate, even to ourselves. As one of my backwoods relatives used to say of her inexplicably ambitious son, "Fritzie wants something what he ain't got at home." We yearn for something we haven't got and what our own finite resources cannot provide—for meaning, for assurance that we matter, for a glimpse of the holy. Our response to this divinely inspired restlessness may lead us down wrong paths and into blind alleys, as we mistake God's tug as a call to ever greater acquisition and achievement or just another avenue to self-improvement. Ultimately, though, we are drawn to the church, "the blessed company of all faithful people," in our yearning for God. Even though at times we might wish otherwise, we need each other. If we are to grow up into Christ, we must recognize that we are part of his body, the church, and that we are expected to accompany one another on the spiritual journey. There is no such thing as a solitary Christian. As Jesus promises in Matthew's gospel, "For where two or three are gathered in my name, I am there among them" (18:20).

Clearly, the church is neither a building nor a bureaucracy, but exists when two or three—or twenty or three hundred—are gathered. Those two or three *are* the church. In other words, church is community. Ideally but not inevitably, this community is the parish. We forget that the word "parish" originally referred to geographical boundaries, denoting an area that contained—among other things—a church building. For many, church and parish are identical. This can mean that they find welcome and nurture there, that they have found their way into the blessed company of all faithful people, or it can mean that they have experienced a community that is rigid, banal, or unloving. I have encountered both extremes, along with considerable well-intentioned mediocrity. Perhaps most painful is my memory of an Anglican parish decades ago when I lived for a year in Argentina. It was not a particularly welcoming place, but I stuck it out, trusting that one day it would feel like the church. The Good Friday sermon decided the issue for me: it was an anti-Semitic diatribe, ending in fervent prayer for the conversion of the Jews. (It could have been worse: we might have prayed for their destruction.) This was the only English-language parish in the community, so I decided that a sabbatical from common worship was permissible.

That was an extreme situation, an experience of the parish church at its worst. Yet its example has stayed with me powerfully: true community is not always found within institutional boundaries. I wish now that I had been more venturesome, but I was a stranger in a strange land with two small children; it was all I could do to cope with everyday household crises in my imperfect Spanish. Looking back, I know that the community of the faithful need not be defined by the walls of a building. Two or three can gather in his name—almost anywhere—to read morning or evening prayer together, to sit prayerfully in silence, or to study scripture. However we go about it, whether we are happily at home in the neighborhood parish or whether previous experience has left us skeptical and disenchanted, we cannot go it alone. It takes at least two or three, gathered in his name.

～ A New Family

Jesus' words to his mother Mary and the beloved disciple spoken from the cross—"Woman, here is your son.... Here is your mother" (John 19:26-27)— are about the creation of a new family, one that transcends biology. At first glance, it would seem that Jesus is commending his mother to the disciple's care: she is stricken and needs someone to look after her. Yet if we look at the picture more closely, we see a relationship of deep mutuality. Mary will bring to it the richness of her years, after a life of joy and sorrow. She knows what it means to put herself aside and to carry God in her heart. She knows the deepest grief of any parent: to watch helplessly as her child suffers and dies. The beloved disciple has the energy and strength of youth, bringing freshness, vision, and openness to risk. Man and woman, younger and older, they complete and complement each other. They do not share the history of ordinary families, which are often fraught with hurt and resentment; rather, they share the history of their love of Jesus and that has brought them together.

This is a family story, but more broadly it is about the creation of new community based on love of God. Like Mary and the beloved disciple, we are given to each other and charged to care for and love another. Our love affair with God is *the* eternal triangle, for it is not possible to love God alone. We are commended to the other family members. After all, when we pray the Lord's Prayer, we are reminded that we are not alone or solitary, but brothers and sisters, mothers and fathers, sons and daughters to one another.

Of course, family analogies are always dangerous. We live in a time when, at least in some circles, the words "family" and "dysfunctional" are almost inextricably linked. The closeness of families is indisputable, even as we spend much of our lives trying to extricate ourselves from that closeness. Nor are we always at our best in our families: my brother is the only person whom I have ever bitten. Yet if we approach it without sentimentality or psychobabble, the family remains a dynamic metaphor for the Christian community.

Biological families are made up arbitrarily, once the parents have—wisely or unwisely—chosen one another. What parent has not heard from a teenager, protesting the restrictions of family life, "I didn't *ask* to be born"? There is no satisfactory parental response to this complaint; we are stuck with each other and our collective baggage. Voluntarily covenanted, the family of the church has more latitude, but also greater responsibility. Unlike the teenager, we cannot complain that we have been thrust into an obtuse and unappreciative circle of people against our will. We have *chosen* to be there, drawn not so much to each other as to Christ as our center. Like Mary and the beloved disciple, we are commended to one another. Our shared love of Christ unites us.

∾ The Crowd Around Jesus

So why does it so seldom seem that way? What keeps us from being a loving family? Matthew, Mark, and Luke all tell a story about Jesus that begins to answer these questions:

> Then his mother and his brothers came; and standing outside, they sent to him and called him. A crowd was sitting around him; and they said to him, "Your mother and your brothers and sisters are outside, asking for you." And he replied, "Who are my mother and my brothers?" And looking at those who sat around him, he said, "Here are my mother and my brothers! Whoever does the will of God is my brother and sister and mother." (Mark 3:31-35)

This is a difficult text to preach on in a suburban parish filled with families of mother, father, and two children, for it sounds as if Jesus is rejecting the human family and repudiating those who have loved him all his life. If we read it as a story about Christ-centered community, however, it leads us to question who and where we are in the picture. Are we those who think we have a special claim on him, standing outside the door and calling to him, or are we part of the crowd, those sitting close to him? In other words, who are the insiders and who are the outsiders?

We tend to be proprietary about our Christian community. To be sure, we have relaxed and become warmer because of the changes introduced in the eucharistically centered 1979 *Book of Common Prayer.* Prior to these liturgical reforms, the neighbor at the crowded communion rail seemed almost an intruder and the reception of the bread and wine an occasion for private devotion. At least in the parishes I frequented in my youth, gentility was a cardinal virtue. Somewhere in a remote dresser drawer I still have my white gloves and little lace doily, which I pinned to the top of my head in lieu of a proper hat. Now I worship in congregations where the exchange of the peace is noisy and prolonged, and the dress code is decidedly relaxed. At one parish especially dear to me, the rector has invited dogs to the eight o'clock service, after realizing that this is the traditional hour for Sunday morning urban dog walkers: "Why not stop in at the church if you're already out and about?" he urged them. The same dogs come faithfully week after week and are remarkably well-behaved, except for an occasional yawn. Their presence has definitely expanded the vision of Christian community at Holy Trinity, and those who are uncomfortable with such inclusiveness are careful to come to a later service.

Well-behaved dogs—and Manhattan pets are a cosseted bunch—might well be more welcome in a typical middle-class parish than some of the men and women who make up the crowd around Jesus. Community, at least on this side of the grave, can be challenging and full of surprises, and Christ can be encountered in unexpected places and found among the wrong kind of people. Sometimes I picture myself, secure in my well-scrubbed Anglican respectability, hanging around outside the door trying to get his attention. "Come with us," I want to say. "We're your real family. Come be with us, where there are no rough edges, where everything is in good taste, where it's *nice*. We'll rescue you from the crowd." But Jesus prefers the crowd.

And what an amorphous, unsettling word it is! A crowd is undifferentiated; it can have all sorts of people in it: joyful, angry, excited, dull, just like us and not like us at all. To be part of a crowd is to let go of any pretense of being special and to let ourselves merge into a larger group. Jesus attracted crowds. They surrounded him, seeking healing and hoping to hear his teaching. They pursued him when he tried to withdraw into solitude and were waiting for him when he returned. (Harried parents know how he must have felt.) Miraculously, he fed them even when there was no food at hand. They lined the road, waving palm branches and shouting "Hosanna," as he rode into Jerusalem. A few days later they shouted, "Crucify him."

In Mark's account of Jesus' true relatives, the crowd is "sitting around him." Perhaps he is teaching or disputing, or perhaps they are just talking. Perhaps they are simply content to be in his presence. We do not know who these people are, whether there are women and children among them, whether there are beggars seeking a handout and sick or deformed people seeking healing. They have followed Jesus home and pressed about him so that he "could not even eat" (Mark 3:20). There is no standard for admission beyond the desire to be with Jesus.

Sometimes in my imagination I restage this story in a typical parish—St. Matthew's will do—on a typical Sunday morning. In his characteristic way, Jesus takes over, and those who think they have the greatest claim on him find themselves standing outside. The people nestled around him do not look as if they belong in the parish. They are dressed all wrong, and they have trouble finding their way around the prayer book—always a litmus test to separate the insiders from the peripheral. Some of the sick ones look as if they might be contagious, and there are a few definitely disturbed ones who have trouble keeping still.

I realize as I write this that I am writing from memory as much as from imagination. As a seminarian I worked for several years in an urban congregation just down the street from a group home for severely retarded adults. One of their counselors began bringing the eight residents to church, even though there were no identified Anglicans among them. For a long time they sat at the back of the church, shushed frequently by their caregiver, working hard at being quiet and meeting standards that must have mystified them. Then one morning at the eucharist Ramon stood up and marched the length of the aisle to the communion rail. He may have been stirred by some vestigial memory, or he may simply have felt the inexorable tug to join the crowd around Jesus. His seven friends trooped along behind him.

It was not quite a scandal—the parish was too genteel and kind for that. But there were whispers: did we know whether they were baptized? If so, had they been confirmed? And after all, how could they understand the significance of what they were doing? I think one person left the parish in protest, but otherwise the presence of the group at the rail gradually ceased to be remarkable, supplanted by new issues and causes of disagreement.

I looked forward to administering the chalice to Ramon and his friends, although I learned to be careful to hold on tightly, for they would greet me with great smiles and reach up to pat my arm or try to hold my hand. Unpredictable and informal as they were, these moments were especially holy. For these people of limited vocabulary, "the Body of Christ, the bread of heaven" and "the Blood of Christ, the cup of salvation" really meant something. They knew that they were receiving much more than a tasteless little starchy disc and a sip of not very good wine. They could never have explained it, but it was clear to me that they were taking God into themselves. This crowd of eight had been drawn to Jesus and may have understood more about his presence than the rest of us. Generously, without any idea of what they were doing, they pulled us all out of the doorway and closer into the warm, vital center.

∽ Signs of a Vital Community
How do we recognize a spiritually vital community? It is not a matter of program, outreach, or great music, al-

though none of these enrichments is to be dismissed. It is more than a roomful of people gathered at ten o'clock on Sunday morning, and more than a roster of the duly baptized, confirmed, and officially recognized communicants of the parish. A spiritually vital community is about members—which Webster defines as "body parts or organs." The letter to the Ephesians has this to say about members of the church:

> But speaking the truth in love, we must grow up in every way into him who is the head, into Christ, from whom the whole body, joined and knit together by every ligament with which it is equipped, as each part is working properly, promotes the body's growth in building itself up in love. (Ephesians 4:15-16)

The author is writing about the Christ-centered community, one that is alive and open to the Spirit, and the openness and loving acceptance of one another that is essential to our life together. Truth and love are not antithetical, but to incorporate them in our care for each other can be hard work.

Truth spoken in love is not ruthless candor, nor is it the facile expression of easy affection. It can even be wordless, but it is deep and faithful. There is no recipe, but it is clear that such discourse is forthright in its childlike simplicity and gentle in its compassion; we learn to discern when speaking will build up the other in love and when it will be destructive. We learn the language of loving silence. Truth spoken in love is rooted in, surrounded, and upheld by Christ's love. It is important to remember this because our own capacity for love may not be enough, indeed sometimes cannot be enough.

In a spiritually vital community we grow up into Christ. Regardless of our chronological age, we are never finished: like growing in social and psychological maturity, growing up into Christ is an ongoing process of conversion. This process can be a source of wonder as we grow up to ever greater simplicity and gentleness and learn to love one another with open hands. In these circumstances, the creation of community is inevitable. We are "joined and knit together": not snapped into place like children's Lego blocks or linked on paper through neat flow charts of responsibility and command, but truly knit into one body. This is a homely image. Broken bones knit as they heal, as the severed parts grow together again. Knitted fabrics are made of a series of connected loops, the resulting material pliant and useful yet at the same time fragile—pulling on one broken stitch can unravel the whole garment. The vital Christian community is more resilient since Christ is the center and the source of energy, binding the members together.

My work takes me into many parishes in the course of a year, and I have learned to take the temperature of the community when I walk in the door as visitor. Openness to the Spirit is simply in the air—or sadly absent. Do people seem to *like* each other? Are they happy to be together again? Do the ushers (and anyone else standing near the door) genuinely greet strangers, or does their idea of welcome mean ensnaring a new warm body? Aggressive tactics of "signing up" newcomers can be off-putting, as can the practice of singling them out for special notice. True warmth in a greeting is, of course, another matter.

The newsletter tells a great deal about a parish. Is it well written, and is it interesting? Does it tell you who is sick or troubled? Does it tell you who is rejoicing—who has a new baby, whose child is going off to college, who has a challenging new job? Is there a sense that people pray for each other? Do you hear more than one voice in the articles? Even the smallest parish can benefit from hearing from someone other than the rector, and there is almost always sufficient literary talent to provide reflections and stories. In the listing of events and outreach programs, is there a sense of frenetic activity, or does it seem a lively community busy in God's vineyard? As a compulsive reader, I peruse a lot of newsletters. Sometimes I think, "I'd like to be with these people, share their lives—not because they are brilliant or successful, but because the love of God shines through them. They are indeed joined and knit together." At other times I think, "No thanks! This makes faithfulness sound like a chore, boring at best and not worth the effort."

It takes more than a good rector to create a vital parish, but thoughtful preaching and good pastoring are essential. Is the priest a real human being or an impressive figure better suited for a pedestal, if not a museum? I know from experience that it is easy to hide behind clerical identity: that stiff plastic collar confers a great deal of power and invites a lot of projections. Can the priest distinguish between healthy authority and self-aggrandizing power? Can he accept his authority and remain humble? Can she recognize the gifts of the laity? Too many clergy know the words and not the music: even as they deplore a lack of lay initiative, they hold on jealously to each committee, each program, each decision. By contrast, a vital parish is a mutual enterprise. Just as the gifts and experience of Mary and the beloved disciple complemented each other, so the gifts of both clergy and laity are essential to community well-being. I am uneasy with clergy who demand excessive deference—the "Father says" syndrome—and even more uneasy with laity who willingly relinquish the priesthood conferred on them in baptism.

Sacristies are incredibly revealing about the spiritual vitality of the parish. Unfortunately, most parishioners do not get backstage. If the last moments before a service are frantic and chaotic, something irreplaceable is lost in the liturgy, even though no one can define it precisely. Prayerfulness in those preparing the liturgy is *not* the same as lugubriousness. The atmosphere can be pleasantly matter-of-fact and down-to-earth, but thoughtful and clear about the purpose of worship. A few years ago I was in a large parish talking about the importance of embedding our public observance in prayer, and commented that the last few minutes in the sacristy told a great deal about the spirituality of the parish. As I briefly described the frenzied, impatient rush that is all too common and noted that the frantic scramble almost always communicated itself to the congregation, the associate clergy all laughed and the rector turned purple. At first I regretted that I had spoken perhaps too much truth, but then decided that this was the prerogative of the outsider, especially when the truth was spoken not only in love but also in innocence.

⟿ Our Common Life

At the heart of community is the humble little word "common." Our prayer book is a book of *common* prayer, meaning that it belongs to all of us and is normally used when we come together, as well as being an excellent book of personal devotion. What we hold in common binds us together and cements the gloriously disparate pieces that make up our community.

Members of Christian community, like biological families, dare not take their mutual love for granted. Joined and knit together, we need to treat each other with tenderness and respect, both individually and in groups. We can never be quite sure when we are sitting in the crowd around Jesus and when we have stationed ourselves in the doorway.

We can start by praying for each other. Here the parish newsletter is an invaluable spiritual resource: we can rejoice with the newly baptized, mourn with the bereaved, and have a sense of what is going on in the community during the other hours of the week. Our prayers are real and specific. We live in lively awareness of one another.

Beyond this deceptively simple habit of holding one another in prayer, we can school ourselves to become comfortable with four simple sentences that can hold the "crowd" together. (Incidentally, these are useful for families as well.)

I love you. To be able to say this and mean it is a giant step toward the vision of a community joined and knit together. We have before us the example of God's love, unconditional and prodigal, enduring in spite of our fallibility. Love goes deeper than liking and does not mean blanket approval. To be able to love the community, even as we accept its shortcomings, means that we let go of carping and grumbling and get on with God's work. In his Rule for monasteries, St. Benedict says, "Above all, let not the evil of murmuring appear for any reason whatsoever in the least word or sign. If anyone is caught at it, let him be placed under very severe discipline."[1] Benedict ran a taut ship, with standards perhaps too stringent for the typical parish, but he makes a good point. Perfect love not only drives out fear; it quashes pernicious murmuring as well. We need to love one another and not be ashamed to reveal it.

Please help me. This is a straightforward acknowledgment of need, not a balancing of the account and a collecting of what we think is owed to us. Just as in a true friendship, sometimes we give and sometimes we receive; sometimes we are the petitioners and sometimes the bestowers. While it is more blessed to give than to receive, it is

---

1. *St. Benedict's Rule for Monasteries*, tr. Leonard J. Doyle (Collegeville, Minn.: The Liturgical Press, 1948), 52.

also easier, at least so long as we can be sure that the gift is not too costly. To admit poverty is painful, although all of us, even the most affluent, live through times of spiritual and emotional impoverishment. It takes courage to ask for help, even to ask for the prayers of our friends.

The folk in the nave on Sunday morning can learn much about spiritually vital communities from the Twelve-Step groups down in the church basement on weeknights. Here truth-telling is fundamental, and surely one of the most difficult truths to be told is the fact of the individual's powerlessness. The community is built on the need for help and the willingness to ask for it—from God and from the diverse group sitting on the folding chairs in the basement. It is a crowd with whom Jesus would have been at home.

I'm sorry. One sentence from the forgettable novel *Love Story* has stuck in my mind: Love is never having to say you're sorry. I remember it because it is so very wrong. We need to say that we are sorry again and again, to express our sorrow to God, to the people whom we love and who love us, and sometimes to the people whom we cannot stand. It can be an apology for a wrong we have done or an obligation neglected, but "I'm sorry" can also be a simple expression of compassion. Sometimes these words are all that we can offer.

Obviously, they need to be sincere. We have all encountered the chronic apologizer, a profound irritant in any community. Then too expressions of compassionate regret can be a subtle or not so subtle way of establishing hierarchy: in the guise of sympathy, we can diminish another and claim for ourselves a spurious invulnerability. I do not like being the "identified patient," at least not all the time. Here again, as Aelred says in *Spiritual Friendship*,[2] we "both

---

2. (Kalamazoo, Mich.: Cistercian, 1974), 45.

learn and teach, give and receive, pour out and drink in."
Truth spoken in love is never cheap and rarely easy. It leads
to genuine mutuality and an increase in generosity.

This growth in charity is the inevitable fruit of true
community and perhaps the touchstone for its recognition.
We know that there is plenty, more than enough for all,
and so we can afford to be generous. Unlike the stay-at-
home brother in the story of the prodigal son, we have at
least an inkling of the prodigality of God's love, so we can
welcome the lost sibling even as we tolerate the accompanying faint whiff of the pigpen, relax, and enjoy the feast
together. There is enough for everyone, and besides it does
not really belong to us. We are all guests at the party. Why
not join in the prodigality?

Such generosity, growing out of mutual respect and
tenderness, extends beyond traditional almsgiving, which
is not to minimize the importance of giving of our sub-
stance. We can also be generous with our time and attentiveness. Once we have put a face and a name to the object
of our charity, that person or group can no longer be an object. This is why it is easier to write a check than to buy a
sandwich for a homeless beggar. We need, of course, to do
both. Living in the spirit, in openness to God, leaves us intensely, even painfully open to God's world.

One of my favorite saints knew about the wonder and
the dangers of living in such openness and surrender. I first
encountered Seraphim of Sarov, a holy man of nineteenth-
century Russia, nearly twenty years ago when I stumbled
onto his biography, a barely believable work of hagiogra-
phy. It was a chance meeting, which is perhaps the way the
saints usually find us: I should have been reading something else, but I was procrastinating and let myself be im-
mersed in Seraphim's story. His simplicity and fearlessness
shone through despite the adulation of his biographer, and

I knew that this was a real person, a homely saint. He preferred the life of a solitary, but all sorts of men, women, and animals sought him out. Even bears, those most unsocial and unbiddable beasts, lumbered out of the forest and ate from his hand.

In his gentleness and humility, Seraphim speaks to me about our life together. Intensely aware of his need for solitude, he devoted Wednesdays and Fridays to prayer, not opening the door of his cell when he was in the monastery and hiding in a specially constructed pit behind the stove in his hermitage. But for the rest of the time he was able to be totally available, generous of himself, his attention, and his prayers. He welcomed all who came to him with his customary term of address, "My joy." This is easy to picture when the guests are young, beautiful, and grace-filled. But this was his greeting to *everyone*—the unkempt, shopworn, even menacing people who sought him out. Like Benedict, he received his guests as if they were Christ.

We have gotten uneasy about terms of endearment outside the intimate circle, aware that they can diminish and demean. Yet I find myself wishing for Seraphim's unselfconsciousness, his sure love of all his fellow creatures, and his childlike willingness to express it. I also catch myself, secure in the immunity brought by age, using the term of endearment that was old when I was a child, "Dear heart." I suspect that unconsciously I am trying to be more like Seraphim, although I stop short at interaction with the black bears in our woods.

Seraphim's power lies not so much in his winsomeness, however, as in the compelling insight that informed his life: God's love is contagious. Caught by it and in it, we are transformed and cannot help but spread the contagion. "Have peace in your heart," he said, "and thousands around you will be saved." This is mind-boggling! Yes, of course we grow in charity as we let ourselves be absorbed into the crowd around Jesus. Yes, of course we grow also in awareness of the pain and anguish in the world around us. But Seraphim is telling us that we have been infected with a powerful virus, more mysterious and tenacious than any of the bodily plagues that threaten our world.

We live in fear of contagion. We have relaxed a bit about the AIDS virus; at least most of us know that we will not become infected when we break bread and share the cup. But as viruses and bacteria mutate and new ones appear, we live in awareness that a mysterious, unseen *something* can invade us and destroy us. Please God, we can also live in joyful awareness of Seraphim's divine contagion.

Have peace in your heart; let your heart be open. Meister Eckhart speaks of making an empty space in our hearts where God can dwell. Look at the crowd around Jesus, and greet each one: "My joy." Have peace in your heart, and thousands around you will be saved. It is a revolutionary concept. It might work if we would only try.

Resources

∿ Classic Works on Prayer

In the past twenty years there has been an enormous amount of writing, both good and bad, on the spiritual life. The following list does not pretend to be complete, and readers will notice many gaps. It is simply an attempt to introduce those exploring the spiritual life, perhaps for the first time, to some of the writings that have formed the tradition of Anglican spirituality and prayer over time.

For the classics of the spiritual life, the best place to start is with the Paulist Press series, *Classics of Western Spirituality*, which provides extensive introductions by scholars in the field as well as good notes and bibliographies. Consult their catalog for works by Julian of Norwich, Teresa of Avila, Meister Eckhart, Hildegard of Bingen, John of the Cross, the author of *The Cloud of Unknowing*, Ignatius of Loyola, Catherine of Siena, Francis and Clare, and Walter Hilton. Anglican writers on spirituality are also well represented, including George Herbert, John Donne, John and Charles Wesley, William Law, and Jeremy Taylor.

Another excellent source of works on monastic and contemplative spirituality is Cistercian Publications. An important focus for this press is works by Cistercian authors, notably Bernard of Clairvaux's many writings on scripture and Aelred of Rievaux's *Spiritual Friendship*, but it also publishes a wide range of books on Coptic, Byzantine, Russian, and desert spirituality that are available nowhere else. Cistercian also publishes monastic women writers of the middle ages.

An easy way to introduce yourself and others to these classics of western and eastern spirituality is to sample some of the many small anthologies now available, such as St. Mary's Press' *Companions for the Journey* series and Ave Maria's *30 Days With a Great Spiritual Teacher*, which feature short daily readings from the saints.

～ Twentieth-Century Works on Prayer

Some of Evelyn Underhill's shorter works on prayer are back in print, including *Abba, The Fruits of the Spirit*, and a new edition of *The Life of the Spirit and the Life of Today* with an introduction by Susan Howatch.

Other recommended general books on prayer are William Temple's *Christian Faith and Life*, Simon Tugwell's two paperbacks *Prayer in Practice* and *Living with God*, Anthony Bloom's *Beginning to Pray*, Michael Ramsey's *Be Still and Know*, Ann and Barry Ulanov's *Primary Speech: A Psychology of Prayer*, Kenneth Leech's *True Prayer*, Thomas Merton's *Bread in the Wilderness* and *The Sign of Jonah*, Martin Smith's *A Season for the Spirit*, Nancy Roth's *The Breath of God*, Alan Jones' *The Soul's Journey*, Henri Nouwen's *Genesee Diary*, Annie Dillard's *Holy the Firm*, and Kathleen Norris' *The Cloister Walk*. More specialized books on prayer are mentioned below.

～ Intercession

Ormonde Plater's *Intercession: A Theological and Practical Guide* offers a basic introduction to private and corporate intercession, while Avery Brooke's *Healing in the Landscape of Prayer* explores healing prayer as a form of intercessory prayer in the context of Anglican worship. For those who regularly say the daily office, Forward Movement's *The Anglican Cycle of Prayer* enables you to pray for Anglicans around the world. If you want to practice daily intercessory prayer, the different forms of the Prayers of the People offered in *The Book of Common Prayer* are an excellent place to begin.

~ Ignatian Prayer

Willam Barry's *Finding God in All Things: A Companion to the Spiritual Exercises of St. Ignatius* is a highly readable introduction to Ignatian prayer for beginners. Anthony de Mello, an Indian Jesuit, has drawn creatively on eastern traditions as well as classic Ignatian prayer in his books of spiritual exercises, notably *Wellsprings: A Book of Spiritual Exercises* and *Sadhana: A Way to God; Christian Exercises in Eastern Form.* Also useful is Gerard Hughes' *God of Suprises.*

~ Centering Prayer

A number of translations and editions of the classic texts on centering or contemplative prayer are available today, including *The Cloud of Unknowing* and others in Paulist Press' *Classics of Western Spirituality.* Modern guides to centering prayer include Thomas Keating's *Finding Grace at the Center,* John Main's *Word Into Silence,* and Basil Pennington's *Centering Prayer.* Thomas Merton's *New Seeds of Contemplation* remains an excellent introduction to contemplative prayer, while Basil Pennington explores the practice of praying the rosary in *Praying By Hand.*

~ Lectio Divina

For the beginner, Thelma Hall's *Too Deep for Words: Rediscovering Lectio Divina* is a valuable guide. Equally helpful and dealing more broadly with scripturally based prayer is Martin Smith's *The Word is Very Near You: A Guide to Praying with Scripture*. This book is an engaging invitation to all aspects of prayer, not only *lectio divina*. Norvene Vest has also included a fine overview of *lectio divina* in her book on Benedictine spirituality, *No Moment Too Small: Rhythms of Prayer, Silence, and Holy Reading*.

Roberta Bondi has written several books that she calls "conversations with the early church on prayer," *To Love As God Loves* and *To Pray and To Love*.

~ Praying in the Midst of Ordinary Life

The classic introduction is Brother Lawrence's *The Practice of the Presence of God*, which is available in different editions and formats. Another valuable work on living in the present is Jean-Pierre de Caussade's *The Sacrament of the Present Moment*. Contemporary books on Benedictine spirituality also emphasize the ordinariness and dailiness of prayer, such as Norvene Vest's Benedictine "workbook," *Preferring Christ*, Joan Chittister's *Wisdom Distilled from the Daily*, and Esther de Waal's *A Life-Giving Way*.

Other books about prayer and daily life are Avery Brooke's *Finding God in the World* and her collection of prayers, *Plain Prayers in a Complicated World*, Margaret Hebblethwaite's *Motherhood and God*, Norvene Vest's *Friend of the Soul*, Madeleine L'Engle's *Circle of Quiet* and *The Summer of the Great-Grandmother*, Macrina Wiederkehr's *A Tree Full of Angels*, Margaret Guenther's *Toward Holy Ground*, Annie Dillard's *Pilgrim at Tinker Creek*, and Kathleen Norris' *Dakota*.

∼ Books of Prayers

The variety and number of books of prayers seems endless. Breviaries of religious orders can be a fruitful source of prayers and canticles, such as *The Daily Office* of the Anglican Franciscans, published in England by Mowbray, and St. Augustine's Prayer Book, published by the Order of the Holy Cross in West Park, New York. *The Book of Common Prayer* is a rich and varied source of prayer for Anglicans, particularly the collects in both contemporary and traditional forms, the psalter, and the canticles for morning prayer. *The Oxford Book of Prayer* includes Christian prayers alongside those from other traditions.

A simple and very fruitful method of daily prayer is to subscribe to Forward Movement's *Forward Day By Day* series. These are small, inexpensive pocket-size books of daily meditations on biblical passages, written by a wide variety of Episcopalians and covering several months at a time. They can be read privately or in small groups.

∼ Spiritual Direction

The Practice of Spiritual Direction by William A. Barry and William J. Connally, both Jesuit spiritual directors, remains the standard in the field. Kathleen Fischer's *Women at the Well* concentrates on women and spiritual direction. For Anglicans, good introductions to the topic are Margaret Guenther's *Holy Listening*, Kenneth Leech's *Soul Friend*, Alan Jones' *Exploring Spiritual Direction*, and Tilden Edwards' *Spiritual Friend*.

∼ Sacramental Confession

Reconciliation: Preparing for Confession in the Episcopal Church by Martin L. Smith, SSJE is an excellent book on preparing for confession, especially for those who have never participated before in the rite of reconciliation. It is also a useful source of insight for those who desire a method for periodic self-examination and for those in regular spiritual direction.

ᛜ Retreats

Roger J. Regalbuto's third edition of *A Guide to Monastic Guesthouses* now includes all fifty states and Canada, a wide range of monasteries and convents across the spectrum of Christian traditions, and gives practical information about settings and history, how to get there, accommodation, and donations.

Books describing the retreat experience are not numerous. Henri Nouwen's *Genesee Diary* is a classic account of monastic routine as experienced by an outsider, while Thomas Merton's *The Sign of Jonah* and his series of journals describe it from the inside. Kathleen Norris' *The Cloister Walk* is a contemporary account of a lay woman's experience in a Benedictine monastery.

The new Rule of the Society of St. John the Evangelist, an Anglican religious order for men, is composed of short chapters on all aspects of community life, including leadership, the use of power, poverty, loneliness, and friendship. It offers a fascinating view of a contemporary monastic ethos.

Questions for Group Discussion

~ **Chapter 1: An Introduction to Spirituality**

1. What secular spiritualities do you see reflected in the world around you? Which are the most persuasive or powerful in your own life? In the life of your parish?

2. What areas of your faith have you chosen to leave unexamined? Why? What are some of the risks involved in spiritual growth?

3. In what areas of your faith have you taken risks and experienced growth?

~ **Chapter 2: Prayer as Conversation**

1. What are some helpful ways you have found to quiet the inner and outer voices in your life?

2. In their introduction to prayer, *Primary Speech*, Ann and Barry Ulanov write, "What begins as worry that our pray-

ers are not answered, ends, if we keep on praying, in awe that answers do come. When that happens, we grow cautious about what we pray for." Describe some ways that God has answered you in prayer, whether through words, dreams, people, or events.

3. Turn to Genesis 32:22 and read (or have someone read aloud) the story of Jacob at the River Jabbok. Has such a messenger come into your life? How did you struggle with the messenger and the message? Describe some other ways God speaks to you in prayer.

~ Chapter 3: Varieties of Prayer

Five traditional varieties of prayer are described in this chapter: adoration, thanksgiving, confession, intercession, and petition. Pick one of these and practice it daily for a week. To put your prayers into words, it might help you to turn to the psalter in *The Book of Common Prayer* and use some of the psalms, such as psalm 29 for adoration, psalm 124 for thanksgiving, psalm 32 for confession, psalm 122 for intercession, and psalm 141 for petition. Or you may want to use favorite passages from scripture.

~ Chapter 4: Prayer Through the Centuries

1. This chapter explores traditional methods of prayer: Ignatian meditation, centering prayer, lectio divina, the Jesus Prayer, and praying the daily offices of *The Book of Common Prayer*. Choose one of these traditions of prayer and practice it daily during the week.

2. In the group, discuss your experience of prayer during the week just past. What attracted you to that way of praying? What did you learn from practicing it every day?

3. Which of the traditions of prayer described in this chapter seem to come most easily for you? Which are the most difficult? Why?

∼ **Chapter 5: Practices of Prayer**

The practices we explored in this chapter—reconciliation, spiritual direction, retreats, journaling—all have to do in some way with self-knowledge and discernment in the spiritual life. Many groups have found the following exercise helpful in developing the self-awareness that in turn will nourish our relationship with God.

1. Begin this exercise by looking back over your life so far and identifying ten "stepping stones," important turning points, or milestones. These are the *outwardly* significant events that have shaped your life.

2. Now identify ten more stepping stones, significant *inner* experiences that have shaped your spirituality. There may be some overlap with the first list but, on the other hand, the second list may contain very different milestones that are known to you alone.

3. Take a week to do this exercise. When you meet together as a group, set aside some time in which people may volunteer to discuss the insights they have gained, but make it clear that they may simply remain silent.

～ Chapter 6: Finding God in the Ordinary

1. Where is your "desert cell" in which you find it a challenge to experience the presence of God? Is it your kitchen, your study, your family, or your place of work? What repetitive tasks help you to "practice the presence of God"?

2. How do you feel called? In what ways do you think of the place where you work as a place of calling? Where do you live out your vocation?

3. In what ways is your home and/or family life a place of coming to know yourself and God? In what ways does it impede you?

～ Chapter 7: Parenting and Prayer

1. Can you identify times in your life when an event profoundly changed your sense of prayer and relationship to God? What helped you to grow spiritually during those times?

2. We all have mental images of God that affect the ways we pray. How have the images of God that inform your prayer changed over the years?

3. What are the distractions in your life right now that make it difficult for you to pray?

～ Chapter 8: Learning Simplicity

1. If you were to choose one specific area of your life that you would like to simplify right now, what would it be—your activities? your social life? your possessions?

your finances? How would you go about it? What is keeping you from starting?

2. What would it mean for you to simplify your speech?

3. For a period of a week, create a small "sabbath" by wasting some time every day. Does this practice of simplicity become easier or harder as the week goes by?

∼ Chapter 9: Praying Through Desolation

1. Many of the psalms speak of our relationship with God in the midst of desolation and despair. During the week make one of these psalms your own by reading and reflecting on it daily. Psalms to consider are pss.10, 13, 42, 55, and 88. What does the psalm tell you about who God is? About who we are?

2. What are your chief places of waiting? What have been some of the significant waiting periods in your life?

3. How have these times of waiting been occasions for spiritual growth? Can you perceive the Good News in your times of desolation?

∼ Chapter 10: Praying in Community

1. One of the collects for Good Friday is a prayer for the community of the church: "O God of unchangeable power and eternal light: Look favorably on your whole Church, that wonderful and sacred mystery...." (BCP 280). Read and reflect on the collect in a group. Where in your church do you see that "things which were cast down are being

raised up, and things which had grown old are being made new"?

2. When you think back to all the various communities of faith in which you have prayed over the years, describe the ones in which you felt you grew the most in prayer and fellowship? In what ways were they "intercessory" communities?

3. What are some of the ways in which communities of faith weaken or undermine our life of prayer?

COWLEY PUBLICATIONS is a ministry of the brothers of the Society of Saint John the Evangelist, a monastic order in the Episcopal Church. Our mission is to provide books and resources for those seeking spiritual and theological formation. COWLEY PUBLICATIONS is committed to developing a new generation of writers and teachers who will encourage people to think and pray in new ways about spirituality, reconciliation, and the future.